GOD ON PSYCHEDELICS
TRIPPING ACROSS THE RUBBLE OF OLD-TIME RELIGION

DON LATTIN

APOCRYPHILE
PRESS

THE APOCRYPHILE PRESS
PO Box 255
Hannacroix, NY 12087

Copyright © 2023 by Don Lattin
ISBN 978-1-958061-28-2 / paperback
ISBN 978-1-958061-29-9 / ebook

Portions of this book were previously published by the author online at *www.lucid.news* and are used here with permission.

All rights reserved. No part of this book may be reproduced, stored in a retrieval system, or transmitted in any form or by any means—electronic, mechanical, photocopy, recording, or otherwise—without written permission of the author and publisher, except for brief quotations in printed or online reviews

Visit the author at www.donlattin.com

Please join our mailing list at
www.apocryphilepress.com/free
We'll keep you up to date on all our new releases,
and we'll also invite you to download a FREE BOOK.
Visit us today!

CONTENTS

Other Books By Don Lattin	vii
Introduction	ix
1. Psychedelic Baptisms	1
2. On Being Psychedelic and Jewish	33
3. Mystic Christian Revelation	53
4. Psychedelic Chaplains	74
5. Ayahuasca Churches Emerge	89
6. Sacred Garden Church	109
7. Psychedelics in Recovery	127
Conclusion	145
Notes	167
Acknowledgments	171

The eye through which I see God
is the same eye through which God sees me;
my eye and God's eye are one eye,
one seeing, one knowing, one love.

—Meister Eckhart, 1260-1328,
Dominican priest and accused heretic

OTHER BOOKS BY DON LATTIN

SHOPPING FOR FAITH
American Religion in the New Millennium
(with Richard Cimino) (Jossey-Bass Publishers, 1998)

FOLLOWING OUR BLISS
How the Spiritual Ideals of the Sixties Shape Our Lives Today
(HarperCollins, 2003)

JESUS FREAKS
A True Story of Murder and Madness on the Evangelical Edge
(HarperCollins, 2007)

THE HARVARD PSYCHEDELIC CLUB
How Timothy Leary, Ram Dass, Huston Smith and Andrew Weil
Killed the Fifties and Ushered in a New Age for America
(HarperCollins, 2010)

DISTILLED SPIRITS
Getting High, then Sober, with a Famous Writer,
a Forgotten Philosopher and a Hopeless Drunk
(University of California Press, 2012)

CHANGING OUR MINDS
Psychedelic Sacraments and the New Psychotherapy
(Synergetic Press, 2017)

INTRODUCTION

There's nothing like a high-dose trip on magic mushrooms, LSD or ayahuasca to get one wondering about this thing we call "consciousness." What is it? Where is it? And why is it so hard to retain, explain and learn from the insights these drugs reveal once we return to our old patterns of thinking? When we transcend our skin-encapsulated egos and connect in new ways to a power greater than ourselves, what is that force we perceive? Is it God, a delusion, or something in between? Is this a "higher self" or a "true self" or is it all just a mental projection? Is this all inside our heads, or are we tuning into some cosmic reality?

Psychedelics are going mainstream. Groundbreaking clinical trials show that mind-altering agents like psilocybin and MDMA can be effective tools to help therapists treat depression, trauma and substance abuse. Cities across the country have decriminalized magic mushrooms and plant-based psychoactive elixirs like ayahuasca, and the states of Oregon and Colorado have legalized and regulated supervised sessions using psilocybin, the active ingredients in those fantastic fungi. Venture capitalists and other investors have poured billions of dollars into start-up companies hoping to get in on the ground floor of The Next Big Thing.

This book seeks to go beyond the commodification and medicalization of psychedelics—past that media hype and the naive exuberance that has fueled much of the "psychedelic renaissance."

I'm asking other questions:

How does the psychedelic revival fit into the larger story of religion in America?

What's God got to do with it?

I've been writing about (and experiencing) chemically induced altered states of consciousness since the 1970s—first as the religion reporter for daily newspapers in San Francisco and more recently as the author of several books on psychedelic spirituality.

It's no secret that psychedelics often inspire profound mystical experiences, even among people who previously considered themselves atheists or long ago fell away from organized religion. These plants, fungi and chemical compounds have the power to deconstruct our pre-conceived ideas about the nature of reality and how we relate to ourselves and the world around us.

My work as a religion journalist and my own psychedelic exploration makes me wonder about a few things:

> Why do relatively few people in the burgeoning psychedelic renaissance connect drug-induced spiritual states with their own religious tradition?

What lessons can mainstream churches and synagogues learn from psychedelic mysticism and the broader "spiritual but not religious" movement in the United States?

What can the religious establishment teach entheogenic explorers about ethics, accountability and community?

God on Psychedelics takes the reader into some of the emerging spiritual communities rising out of a new wave of psychedelic practice. It also looks at an avant-garde of mainstream clergy who see entheogenic exploration as one way to deepen the experiential faith of Christian and Jews.

Even before the ravages of the COVID pandemic, churches and religious denominations in the United States faced sharp declines in attendance and affiliation. This book does not claim that magic mushrooms or ayahuasca have the power to miraculously revive organized religion in America. But their burgeoning popularity and public acceptance are already fueling the rise of alternative communities of spiritual seekers moving beyond the tired dogma, divisive doctrine and outdated denominationalism of old-time religion. Psychedelics will not save the world, but when used responsibly they can show us another way, opening us up to our own innate sources of love, awareness, wisdom, grace, gratitude and connection.

This book is based on dozens of interviews with psychedelic guides, people of faith and people who've lost their faith. We'll hear from some extraordinary folks who've thought deeply about the interplay between chemically assisted mysticism,

Judaism and Christianity. But first, let me place my own tarot cards on the table. Like many baby boomers coming of age in the 1960s and 1970s, I had a few revelatory and existentially challenging experiences on drugs like LSD, peyote, MDA and magic mushrooms. Psychedelics blew away what I once saw as "reality," opening my mind to profound unitive experiences with the natural world and other members of my entheogenic (seeking the divine within) tribe. These powerful substances also revealed the darker sides of my soul. They did not prevent me from falling to periods of soul-numbing depression, temporary psychosis and substance abuse.[1]

In the beginning, I thought very little about how these mystical experiences of heaven and hell connected with the faith of my Jewish grandmothers and Protestant forefathers. But in more recent years, I've gone through my own little psychedelic renaissance. This time around, I've started to look at how the triumphs and traumas of my ancestors made me into the person I am today and how they set the stage for my love/hate relationship with organized religion.[2]

Psychedelics helped sparked my career as the longtime religion writer at the *San Francisco Chronicle*. They inspired me to explore Zen meditation, shamanism, Taoism and t'ai chi. For that we can credit or blame such leading lights as Aldous Huxley, Alan Watts, Timothy Leary, Richard "Ram Dass" Alpert, Ralph Metzner, Carlos Castaneda and, later, Terence McKenna.

In more recent times, open-minded Christians like the late Huston Smith, the Methodist minister and professor of comparative religion, and Brother David Steindl-Rast, the Benedictine monk and Catholic interlocutor to the "spiritual but not religious" cohort, showed me another way to look at the lapsed Protestantism of my paternal tribe. Jewish scholars like the rabbis Adin Steinsaltz and Arthur Green cracked open the long-repressed Judaism of my maternal ancestors—Russian Jews chased to New York by the czar and his ministers.

God on Psychedelics does not seek to promote drug use or proselytize any religion—neither Judaism, Christianity, nor perennialism, animism or syncretism, that amorphous mix of spiritual traditions one finds in so much of today's psychedelic movement. But it does seek to understand all of these spiritual expressions in a deeper way, through the prism of altered states of consciousness.

My spiritual path and journalist approach is that of a skeptical universalist. By that I mean someone who seeks to find truth in the world's religions, but one who is also on the lookout for the hypocrisy, divisiveness and grandiosity that seems to corrupt them all.

There are many reasons for the sharp decline in church membership and attendance in the United States over the past fifty years. Political battles over feminism, abortion and gay rights have divided churches just like they have in the larger culture. Today, much of the evangelical movement has aligned itself with messianic nationalists and the right-wing agenda of the Republican Party. Meanwhile, millions of Roman Catholics have become disillusioned with their own leadership, including pontiffs and prelates who spent decades covering up the sexual abuse of children and teenagers by priestly hypocrites.

America's old "mainline" churches—including relatively progressive denominations like those representing Methodists, Lutherans, Presbyterians and Episcopalians—have been shunted to the sidelines. Their ongoing decline comes at the expense of the fastest growing religion in America—the so-called "Nones" and those who call themselves "spiritual but not religious." These are folks who have left organized religion, but still believe in God or some more amorphous higher power

—or feel somehow connected to a mystical "ground of being." They may not be filling churches every Sunday to recite the Nicene Creed, but they have joined other small groups devoted to spiritual exploration—meditation groups, yoga classes, Bible study circles, twelve-step recovery fellowships, men's groups, women's groups, and, yes, psychedelic churches. These are seekers more interested in cultivating religious *experience* than they are in reciting religious *belief*. And, as those who've been there know, nothing blows away belief and fuels powerful spiritual encounters like a high-dose trip on such entheogens as LSD, magic mushrooms, ketamine or DMT.

At the same time, the psychedelic movement, including some of those leading its renaissance, has already left the Garden of Eden. Many have given in to the "powers and principalities" of the world. Just like in the larger culture, today's psychedelic community is torn apart by political infighting, allegations of sexual abuse and the temptations of the almighty dollar. In a saga similar to the story of cannabis in America, drugs like magic mushrooms and MDMA are being medicalized as one step on the road to legalization. Some powerful players seek to have them commodified and politically controlled by a new class of high priests, physicians and psychotherapists.

Over the last decade, I have spent countless hours talking to scientists, spiritualists, philosophers and diehard psychonauts. I have drunk ayahuasca in the jungles of Brazil, smoked toad venom with heroin addicts at a Mexican treatment center, toured a Swiss neuroscience lab, joined a psychedelic church and helped start a twelve-step organization dedicated to the proposition that psychedelics can give some alcoholics the spiritual awakening we need to truly recover from our affliction. And, after all that, there are moments when I finding myself stepping back, shining the harsh spotlight of skepticism onto all of the above. Are we just "getting high?" There's little question in my mind that psychedelic drugs, used with caution and respect, can provide therapeutic and spiritual benefit. At the time same, they can fool us into believing practically anything. These are trickster drugs. Possible side effects include the tendency to believe that reality is just a collective hunch.

One wonders what the late Huston Smith, the renowned scholar of the world's religions, would have to say about the current state of psychedelia. In the opening years of the 1960s, Huston was an early supporter and associate of Timothy Leary, the clinical psychologist who left Harvard to become the self-proclaimed "high priest" of the 1960s counterculture. Smith soon soured on the free-wheeling social and spiritual crusade launched by Leary, Alpert, Ken Kesey and his band of Merry Pranksters.[3] Smith wondered whether these altered states of consciousness produced altered traits of human behavior. Do these flashes of illumination produce the abiding light of a religious life? Not really, he concluded. In an article published in 1967 in the journal *Christianity and Crisis*, Smith announced that he was stepping back from his "initial, rather optimistic appraisal of the promise entheogens ('God-enabling' drugs) hold for religion."

One of the things we did learn in the 1960s, and need to remember today, is that the psychedelic experience has everything to do with "set and setting." Today's psychonauts have different definitions of "set and setting," but here's mine: What are our intentions, our mindset, going into a trip? How do we integrate whatever revelations we might have into our daily lives. Back in the day, too many of us were too quick to throw out the old road maps—the wisdom and the mysticism of our Jewish and/or Christian heritage.

Huston, who died in 2016, questioned his optimistic

assessment of psychedelics more than half a century ago. It's time to take another look, to reexamine the question: What promise and potential do entheogens hold for a new generation of spiritual seekers and for the crumbling infrastructure of American religion?

CHAPTER 1
PSYCHEDELIC BAPTISMS

Living Grace Lutheran Church, a struggling congregation on the outskirts of Omaha, seems like the last place for an experiment into the redemptive power of psychedelic spirituality. Nebraska is one of the most politically and culturally conservative states in America—a place where both medical and recreational marijuana are still illegal. Bringing a single edible gummy across the border from Colorado remains a felony offense in Nebraska. Yet, in a quiet way, Living Grace's pastor, the Rev. James Lindberg, found himself playing a key role in one of the more unusual research projects of the burgeoning psychedelic renaissance.

Most of the studies underway at universities and medical centers from New York to San Francisco examine the potential mental health benefits of psychedelic-assisted therapy. Can MDMA, known on the street as "Ecstasy" or "Molly," help treat military veterans or rape victims suffering from Post Traumatic Stress Disorder? Can psilocybin, the psychoactive ingredient that puts the magic in those mushrooms, assist in the treatment of depression or substance abuse?

Rev. Lindberg was a volunteer in a very different kind of experiment by psychedelic therapy researchers at the Johns Hopkins University School of Medicine in Baltimore and NYU Langone Health in Manhattan. He was one of two dozen healthy and "psychedelically naive" religious professionals—rabbis, priests, seminary professors—who participated in a (as of this writing) yet-to-be published study.

After careful screening and preparation, each were separately given two doses of synthesized psilocybin in a comfortable, supervised setting. The idea was to measure whatever chemically induced mystical experiences they might have had and follow-up to see how that divine encounter helped—or hindered—them in their ministry. At first glance, this might sound like the setup for an irreverent joke. *A rabbi, Catholic priest and a Protestant preacher walk into a room and are given a hefty serving of magic mushrooms.* But it wasn't a gag, and what happened next was anything but irreverent.

This chapter recounts the magical mystery trips of four of those research subjects—all of them Protestant clergy. Two had mostly positive experiences and left feeling more inspired in their ministry.

"It's surprising how many clergy have never had a mystical experience," said the Rev. Roger Joslin, who shepherds two Episcopal churches on Long Island, New York. "How are you going to incorporate mystery into the life of your congregation if you don't know what that's like yourself?"[1]

"Institutional religion has a lot to learn from psychedelics," said the Rev. Hunt Priest, an Episcopalian who has gone on to start an organization to assist other clergy and lay people interested in entheogenic exploration. "And the psychedelic community has a lot to learn from organized religion."[2]

Two other study participants, including James Lindberg, initially left feeling more confused than enlightened.

The Rev. Rita Powell, an Episcopal minister and Harvard chaplain, was left wondering why she didn't encounter Christ on her journey. "I entered a space of nothing. There was no space to enter. I saw no one. I was nowhere. There was neither color, nor its absence. There was no form, nor its absence. There was not fear. There was not joy. There was not revelation. There was nothing."[3]

Psychedelics, said Lindberg, initially left this Lutheran pastor with something that could be called a "crisis of faith."

"They cracked me open and showed me that my views of the world were small and limited, compared to what I had just experienced. For a while, I struggled with what it means to be an identified member of the clergy who is supposed to promulgate the doctrines of that religion. I became more humble when I spoke about God. God is bigger and more vast than I can wrap my head around."[4]

THE NEW WAVE of entheogenic exploration in the United States comes amid a historic decline in church attendance, a free fall that began before the COVID pandemic. According to a Gallup poll, membership in houses of worship dropped below fifty percent in 2020 for the first time in eight decades of surveying. Only forty-seven percent of those polled reported membership in a church, synagogue or mosque, down from seventy percent in 1999.

Lindberg's denomination, the Evangelical Lutheran Church in America (ELCA), has been especially hard hit. Membership is falling so fast that—according to one projection this mainline denomination will be on the verge of extinction in one or two generations.[5] As a young reporter on the "religion beat," I covered the 1987 convention in Columbus,

Ohio, when three smaller Lutheran denominations voted to merge into the new 5.3-million-member ELCA. By the year 2020, national membership had dropped to 3.1 million members.

James Lindberg, born in 1970, was raised in a family of Lutherans in Sacramento, California. His middle name is "Christian." Growing up, he thought about becoming a police officer, a social worker or a high school teacher. But after getting an undergraduate degree at Sacramento State University, Lindberg found himself enrolled at Luther Seminary in St. Paul, Minnesota, in the heartland of American Lutheranism. "There were no grand epiphanies or spiritual experiences that led me to the ministry," he recalled. "Church was just something that was very familiar to me. I went into ministry because the church was a good fit for me. I just love the church."

In 2008, he was assigned by the Evangelical Lutheran Church in America to plant a new church in the growing suburbs west of Omaha. "We were going to build a big building and be a traditional Lutheran church—maybe even a mega-church if we played our cards right and read enough Steven Covey books," said Lindberg, referring to the best-selling self-help author and management consultant.

Pastor Lindberg started his ministry just as declining attendance was hitting churches across the country. Meeting in rented space in a high school auditorium, the congregation grew to about 125 in weekly worship. Then it fell to 100, then 90, and then COVID hit. "We now get about 20-25 people in person," he said, "plus about 10-15 online."

In 2018, Lindberg was reading a digest of religion news when he saw a dispatch with the headline, "Religious Leaders Take Magic Mushrooms." While he'd never taken psychedelics before, he'd smoked some marijuana a few years earlier in

Colorado, where cannabis is legal, and saw that "there was a spiritual aspect to it."

In the Johns Hopkins study, religious professionals who qualified for the experiment were given two opportunities to trip out on psilocybin. It was the usual set-up in the new wave of clinical trials—a living room-type setting, eye shades, evocative music and two guides to oversee the journey.

"It was a unitive experience," Lindberg recalled. "A loss of self and boundaries and identifying roles—male, pastor, husband—becoming singular in my experience of me rather than my roles…It sounds hokey, but it felt like a soul journey, a journey of the spirit. It was like getting into a little boat and going out into the cosmic ocean. There were storms. There was beauty. There were neon green gardens and a city of clouds, but I wasn't so interested in that, but more into moving into a unitive space."

In a Zoom interview, I asked Lindberg if there was anything "Christian" about his two trips. "Not anything, really," he replied.

"They showed me something about what is truth and what is reality and what it means to be a person of faith with all the doctrines and beliefs of the church and the hierarchy and structure and powers. The psychedelic experience deconstructed a lot for me. I can see why a government would want to see these things suppressed. Not because people are going to fry their minds but, at least for me, they deconstructed culture. They deconstructed belief."

In the end, like so many other mainline Protestant congregations in America, Living Grace Lutheran Church did not make it. One year after our first interview, on February 26, 2023, the congregation held its final Sunday worship service. The church—one of hundreds of Lutheran congregations to die off over the last decade—became another statistic in the crumbling infrastructure of old-time religion. Among the reasons cited for this decline are aging congregations, divisive politics and a lack of interest among people who call themselves "spiritual but not religious." Then COVID and temporary church shutdowns changed people's Sunday habits, pounding the final nails into the ecclesiastical coffin. The good news—at least for this 52-year-old pastor—is so few young people are entering Lutheran ministry that James expected to have little trouble finding a new position.

While Lindberg does not see salvation in psychedelics, he told me his sessions at Johns Hopkins changed his approach to ministry in subtle-yet-significant ways. "I became more of a chaplain in my approach to people," he said. "Rather than trying to teach people how their faith should be, I became more open to how they see God and how they see the faith. I'm not telling them what God thinks. It's much more about listening to how their faith is a resource for them and working to support them in their understanding of God."

UNLIKE JAMES LINDBERG, the Rev. Roger Joslin is a second-career pastor. Born in Texas in 1951, he spent the first two decades of his professional life crafting customized cabinets and wood trim. "Very high-end stuff for people with too much money," he quipped. "Texans tend to be rather ostentatious. They like to show their wealth."

Joslin was brought up in the conservative evangelical Southern Baptist Convention, the nation's largest Protestant denomination. In 1969, that church refused to support him is his opposition to the war in Vietnam and his decision to seek conscientious objector status. "I decided they didn't take what

Jesus taught as seriously as I did," he said, "so I left the church."

Looking back, Joslin sees that he "always had a spiritual bent," but it was a connection he found in the natural world—hiking, running, canoeing and cycling. In the late 1990s, he was camping in the spectacular Sangre de Cristo Mountains in northern New Mexico and running on trails behind the Pecos Benedictine Monastery. Fearing that he might get lost, he laid sticks down at a few crossroads to show him the way back. Upon his return, he noticed that they formed a cross.

"So, in a literal way," he said, "the cross was showing me the way back to the monastery."

Conversations there with one of the monks, Brother Patrick, convinced him to begin the long process of entering seminary and seeking ordination as an Episcopal priest. After graduating from the Episcopal Theological Seminary of the Southwest in 2005, Joslin was sent to Bentonville, Arkansas, the hometown of Wal-Mart, to start an Episcopal church. After ten years there, he was transferred to the eastern end of Long Island and assigned to two parishes in Mattituck and Greenport.

He heard about the Johns Hopkins experiment when Hunt Priest, one of his best friends from seminary, sent him a photo of an advertisement that the researchers had placed in *Christian Century* magazine, seeking volunteers. "This has your name all over it," Priest said.

His two psilocybin journeys were very different, but profound in their own ways. "The first journey was magical and mysterious and grand," he said. "I visited other worlds. I saw a glimpse of another universe. I had an experience of theological unity that I had accepted for a long time—that we are all one, that creation is of one substance. I believed that, but after my first psilocybin experience, I knew it to be true. I felt it in my bones. I was whisked away to these other planets and interesting places and seeing all kinds of things I couldn't imagine. It was exhausting and frightening, then I would find myself in this place of restoration. It was like a garden or a market full of fruit and pastries and candies. They were served by beautiful women who were kind and generous—a place of abundance and healing.

"The second time very different. I was in the throes of a divorce and my mother had died. I just cried and cried for what felt like hours...It felt like years of psychotherapy. I said goodbye to my wife and mother and to every person I had ever lost. It was beautiful and horrible... So one journey was very mind expanding and the other very therapeutic, but both very powerful and important."

Neither Joslin nor Lindberg talked about their experiences with their congregations—just with their bishops and a few clergy friends. Nevertheless, Joslin sees a time in the not-so-distant future when psychedelically induced mystical experiences will be offered to congregants who wish to have the experience. Not as a substitute for Holy Communion, but at church retreats overseen by trained guides. "I think the church ought to be part of this," he said. "We need to play a role in the most mystical experience people are ever going to encounter. Churches are dying. This could revitalize the church.

"There are all kinds of ways of having a mystical experience —meditation, deprivation of one kind or another, breathwork, dreams. Our scripture is riddled with mystical experiences. It's what religion at its base is all about. As an outgrowth from that, we care about the poor, we care about justice. But anybody can do that...Right now, it's not legal so there are limited things we can do with it. But at some point, the psychedelic experience can be incorporated with these other mystical pathways to the divine."

Joslin said his psychedelic experiences at Johns Hopkins instilled a new spirit into his Sunday liturgies. He was overseeing two parishes and doing four services every Sunday morning.

Before his psychedelic journeys, he feared that "the celebration of the Eucharist would become trite and meaningless." Afterward, "the Eucharist turned into a kind of mantra. By the fourth time on Sunday, I was in a different place. The residual effects stayed with me for a year. It affected me as a priest, and the liturgy now is more powerful than it's ever been."

HUNT PRIEST UNDERWENT a similar revival following his two trips at Johns Hopkins. "I had a very Pentecostal experience the first time—feeling my body, speaking in tongues. I felt a force of energy blow into my body," he recalled. "Now I see that spiritual healing is real. I'd laid hands on people and prayed with people, but frankly, I was just touching and holding space. Now I know healing is real. It's a little embarrassing to admit it, but I was in my head all the time. This was in my body...I *did* experience the Holy Spirit. I'm clear about that. I felt like my journey at Hopkins was a second ordination."

His experience was so powerful that—with the permission of his church superiors—he left his parish at St. Peter's Episcopal Church in Savannah, Georgia, and started a new Christian psychedelic society. He calls it Ligare, from the same Latin root that gives us the word "ligament," meaning to bind and unite. "Religion at its best," he explained, "binds us to God."

With seed money from the Riverstyx Foundation, Priest was able to get Ligare off the ground. The organization describes itself as "a collaborative community of clergy, religious educators, scholars, spiritual guides, philanthropists and psychedelic researchers dedicated to making direct experience of the sacred available to all who desire it through the responsible legal use of psychedelic medicine and within the context of Christian contemplative practice."

Priest grew up in a small town outside Lexington, Kentucky, attending the Disciples of Christ church. Like Joslin, he sought Christian ordination as a second career, following nine years working in advertising for Delta Airlines. He spent eight years as a minister in Seattle, before transferring to his parish in Savannah.

Like in James Lindberg's Lutheran denomination, the membership and attendance decline in the Episcopal Church are so severe that some informed insiders have likened this church community to an endangered species. National membership has dropped from 3.4 million in the 1960s to 1.8 million in 2019. And that was *before* the COVID pandemic. "At this rate," one expert predicted, "there will be no one in worship by around 2050 in the entire denomination."[6]

Hunt Priest is not so naive to think that psychedelics will save the Episcopal Church, but at this point, what do church leaders have to lose? "I have a clear sense that this is my ministry going forward," he said. "The church is never going to be the same, and it shouldn't be the same…I hope we can carve out a niche for non-clinical religious use of psychedelics. Religion has something to offer—a container, a vessel, and a documented history of mystical experiences."

FOR RITA POWELL, the Episcopal priest and Harvard chaplain, participating in the Hopkins/NYU study was part of her larger search for a divine presence, a belief that "there is more to the world than meets the ordinary waking eye." As a Christian, she understood that presence through the words of Jesus, the Apostle Paul and the gospel story of incarnation. "The idea that God dwells in our bodies is something that should, and can, radically change how we experience our bodies, and therefore, the rest of the world." Many of us are "trapped in a small reality that we have created."

Perhaps psychedelics could crack open that small reality, that limited sense of self. Or maybe not. "Mainstream Protestant Christianity, of which the Episcopal Church is a part, does not look favorably on drug use, and certainly not from its clergy," she said. "It's viewed as a cheat, a shortcut, and maybe doesn't even really deliver the divine, but some kind of chemical fantasy."

Powell was both curious and put off by the pre-trip vision put forth by one of her guides, that her psilocybin experience would be positive, unitive and beautiful. "It seemed like kind of sloppy, hippie stuff about love and harmony. I didn't need drugs to know about love and harmony and God's presence in the world."

But curiosity trumped skepticism and Powell eventually found herself entering the session room at NYU. She wore a sacred shawl and carried an eagle feather made from a buffalo rib, a gift from people she had previously ministered to in South Dakota. As she came onto the drug, she began to cry. "I wept for my children, whom I could not protect from the sorrow of existence."

Her entry in the void, described in her earlier quote, left Powell exhausted. Her eyes felt like they'd melted shut. There was a crushing weight on her chest. She clutched the hand of her guide, focused on her breath, and made it through the terror. She now looks back on the experience as "maybe the hardest thing I had done in my life."[7]

She was also left with a lot of questions. "What did the

experience tell me about what I thought I knew of God? Why hadn't I met Christ? Did that mean I was outside of Christianity? Had I died in some way? Was that a preview of the absolute emptiness of the other side?"

Her questions inspired a deeper exploration into the rich history of Christian mysticism. There was the Gospel of Thomas, a text dating back to the earliest decades of the church. There were the writings of Saint John of the Cross, the sixteenth century Spanish priest. *To reach satisfaction in all, desire satisfaction in nothing. To come to the knowledge of all, desire the knowledge of nothing. To come to possess all, desire to possess nothing. To arrive at being all, desire to be nothing.*

"It turns out," she said, "that this experience did not put me outside of Christianity, but more deeply inside."

WHAT LESSONS CAN we learn from the mystical experiences of this Protestant quartet?

First of all, they remind us that organized religion views mysticism—whether or not it is occasioned by psychedelic drugs—as both a blessing and a curse. Scholars of religion call this "the institutionalization of charisma." It's one thing for Jesus of Nazareth to have his awakening—forty days in the wilderness, temptation by the devil—and then be inspired to critique the hypocrisies of the religious leaders of his day. It is something else when latter-day mystics, prophets and would-be messiahs arise in the following generations and centuries. The early Christian sect that organized around the Gospel of Thomas (more on this later) was brutally repressed by church leaders who refused to put that gospel story into what became the New Testament. Saint John of the Cross—the child of Jews forced to convert to Christianity during the Spanish Inquisition

—is now canonized and considered one of the "doctors of the church." But in his day he was imprisoned by religious authorities threatened by his reforms.

There is also the long history of the church demonizing sacred plant medicines, whether they be potions used by women condemned as witches or sacraments employed by indigenous tribes. Between 1620 and 1779, the Mexican franchise of the Spanish Inquisition worked tirelessly to suppress the use of mushrooms and peyote, which it condemned as "devilish roots." Heresy hunters prosecuted scores of *curanderos* who used mescaline-containing cacti to fuel clairvoyance, diagnose illness, predict the weather and bewitch their enemies. We'll explore this bloody history in a later chapter, but we can draw a straight line between the church's crusade against entheogens and the global "war on drugs."[8]

Given all this history, it's not surprising that the researchers at Johns Hopkins and NYU had a hard time finding two dozen volunteers for their psilocybin experiments. Members of the clergy approach psychedelics with the same preconceived ideas as other people. This little experiment also reminds us that the most powerful and potentially transformative experiences one has on psychedelic drugs are often on our initial high-dose trip. This radical realignment of our sense of self may give the baptized psychonaut their first taste of a "non-dual" state of consciousness. We are blasted beyond our normal subject/object, us-versus-them state of mind. We suddenly see—or at least we think we see—how everything is connected. This can produce intense feelings of gratitude, love, awe and wonder. We may say things like "this is how one ought to see." This may force us, like James Lindberg, to re-examine our old roles, beliefs and rules for living.

Others—like Hunt Priest—may tune into bodily energy for the first time in our lives. So many of us live in our heads.

Psychedelics have the power to put us in touch with our hearts and the rest of our bodies. They can also blow away the sense that our skin is the boundary between ourselves and the rest of the world. That can be liberating or terrifying. That's why it's so important to be prepared for the experience and have a seasoned guide to accompany initiates and reassure them that everything will be okay.

High dose psychedelics can produce a kind of ego dissolution, inspiring us to be less self-centered and more open-minded. Witness Rev. Lindberg's revelation that he is now more likely to listen to the actual life experiences of his congregants, rather tell them what the church believes about God.

On the other hand, psychedelics also have the power to do the opposite. They can instill fear, paranoia and what feels like psychosis. They can fuel grandiosity and messianism. *I am the center of the world and can save it with psychedelics.* It's not hard to see this in the psychedelic movement—both among the pioneers in the 1950s and 1960s and among those who are now mainstreaming what took root in the counterculture.

In the early 1960s, Timothy Leary and Richard Alpert, later known as Ram Dass, launched a crusade to turn America on to LSD after they were kicked out of Harvard. At one point, they even talked about putting it in the water supply. In the 2020s, young venture capitalists and high-tech entrepreneurs are launching a new brand of Big Pharma—hoping to patent new psychedelic potions, save the world, *and* make a small fortune.

One of the things that impressed me about these four psychedelic initiates was that they are taking these lessons and moving slowly and cautiously. They did not return to their pulpits and start preaching about psychedelics. They know that most of the members of their flocks are probably not that interested in mysticism—whether it is induced with a pill, or spiritual retreat where the mystical vehicle is meditation or contemplative prayer. Most people turn to the church for a sense of community, greater purpose, and lessons for living a more ethical and less self-centered life.

My conversations with these pastors took place in early 2022, just before the sixtieth anniversary of an encounter that has come to be revered as a mythic event in the Church of Psychedelic Revelation. It happened on April 20, 1962 and has come to be known as the Good Friday Experiment.

Twenty students from Andover Newton Theological Seminary gathered in a basement chamber known as Marsh Chapel, across the Charles River from Harvard on the Boston University campus. Half the students were given capsules containing thirty milligrams of psilocybin and the other half were given an active placebo containing nicotinic acid, which induces a tingling sensation. It was a "double-blind" study, meaning neither the seminarians nor the researchers running this little experiment knew if they were getting the placebos or the synthesized magic mushroom medicine.

This study was designed by Walter Pahnke, a medical doctor and Protestant minister, as his PhD project at Harvard Divinity School. Timothy Leary—who at first thought the project was a bit of a joke—was one of Pahnke's academic advisors. Leary criticized Pahnke for not first trying psychedelics himself, echoing a debate that continues among psychedelic researchers today, many of whom refuse to discuss their own drug experiences. Leary also mocked the entire notion of using double-blind, placebo-controlled studies to compare and measure mystical experiences. Unlike with some other experimental drugs, pretty much everyone knows who gets the fake pills and who gets the real thing.

In the Good Friday Experiment, also known in psychedelic lore as the "Miracle in Marsh Chapel," all of the seminarians were given questionnaires designed to determine if they had a mystical experience. Did they experience a sense of unity? Did they transcend space and time? Did they experience euphoria, ineffability, unity and a heightened sense of sacredness? Pahnke would later report that eight of the ten students who got psilocybin experienced at least seven of the components of a mystical experience. None of the seminarians who got the placebo had such high scores. In its report on the experiment, *Time* magazine enthusiastically reported that "all of the students who had taken the drug psilocybin experienced a mystical consciousness that resembled those described by saints and ascetics."

Those who were in the room where it happened describe a somewhat more comical and chaotic scene. They had listened to an audio feed coming from the Good Friday worship service in the main sanctuary upstairs—prayers, hymns and a sermon by the Rev. Howard Thurman, a noted African-American preacher who helped inspire the ministry of the Rev. Martin Luther King. But the experiment dragged on for several more hours. Some of the seminarians and supervisors who got the placebo grew bored and annoyed. They spent much of the time laughing at the profound utterances coming from their stoned brethren. "It was the stupidest thing you ever saw in your life," one of them told me decades later. "Guys were crawling around on the floor on their hands and knees."[9] One of them got paranoid and also tried to leave the dungeon-like chapel. Another seminarian was so consumed by messianic fantasies that he actually managed to escape from the chamber and accost a postal worker on Commonwealth Avenue. He had to be dragged back into the church and given a shot of Thorazine to calm him down.

Four years later, in 1966, Pahnke was conducting government-approved psychedelic research at Spring Grove State Hospital in Maryland. It was there that he met a young psychologist named William A. Richards. They co-authored a paper titled "Implications of LSD and Experimental Mysticism." Their academic collaboration and deep friendship would abruptly end in 1971, when Pahnke died in a scuba diving accident at age forty. Richards continued his psychedelic-assisted therapy with alcoholics and cancer patients at the Maryland Psychiatric Research Center until 1977, when politicized, anti-drug hysteria finally shut down their studies.

That year marked the end of some thirty years of research and clinical practice using classic psychedelics like LSD and psilocybin to treat depression, substance abuse and the existential anxiety that often comes with a life-threatening medical diagnosis. That first wave of government-sanctioned, psychedelic-assisted therapy, began in the late 1940s, just a few years after the Swiss chemist Albert Hofmann discovered the powerful psychoactive effects of lysergic acid diethylamide.

Later in his life, Hofmann himself saw the hand of God in that discovery. "LSD was not a product of planned research," he said. "I did not look for it, it came to me. This means to me that a higher authority thought it was necessary now to provide mankind with an additional pharmacological aid for spiritual growth."[10]

Today, Timothy Leary, Richard Alpert and their freewheeling crusade to "turn on" America are often blamed for the government crackdown on LSD—whether as a recreational drug, research chemical, or psychedelic sacrament. There is some truth to that myth, but the real story is more complicated.

Some of the most abusive and unethical research into LSD was conducted by the U.S. government itself through its various intelligence agencies. Revelations about these experiments in the 1950s and early 1960s, designed to see if LSD could be used as a chemical weapon or "truth serum," only came to light in the post-Watergate era thanks to investigations by Congress, public interest lawyers, and the news media. In 1977, the same year the government shut down socially beneficial research at Richards' facility in Maryland, I published one of my first major stories as a young journalist working in San Francisco. It was the lead story of the combined Sunday, October 9 editions of the *San Francisco Examiner and Chronicle,* under the headline, "The Horror of U.S. Army Drug Tests."

Exactly five years before that, in the fall of 1972, I'd conducted my own little series of drug tests as a freshman at the University of California at Berkeley. Two of those journeys—the classic "good trip" and the "bad trip" from central casting—still resonate as my cautionary tale about the agony and the ecstasy of careless psychedelic experimentation. Since I recount that in some detail in a previously published memoir, there's no need to rehash heaven and hell here.[11] But my wondrous trip on the Big Sur coastline, followed a few weeks later by a temporary psychotic break, left me both open to and skeptical of chemically-induced mysticism.

Today's researchers, including those dosing religious professionals at Johns Hopkins and NYU, have also learned some lessons from the past. Yes, their project is in some ways a repeat of the Good Friday experiment. But this time around there is more care given to pre-screening participants, preparing them for the experience, and following up with them to help integrate any revelatory insights into their actual lives. They've abandoned the double-blind, placebo-controlled model. Unlike back in the days of Leary and Alpert, these researchers are not tripping out with their subjects. Two sober guides are present to supervise individual subjects, making sure no one runs out into the street to announce the dawning of the New Age.

Yet, like in the 1960s, much of today's research into psychedelic-assisted therapy remains a social movement in the guise of a scientific experiment. It's no coincidence, for example, that the first rumblings of a Christian psychedelic movement in the 2020s arose from research in Baltimore, not far from where Walter Pahnke and Bill Richards worked in the late 1960s. So, in a sense, the crusade to introduce psychedelics into the religious mainstream has been underway for sixty years—although much of it was forced underground during the "war on drugs" in the 1970s and 1980s.

Some of the Johns Hopkins research dates back to the 1990s and the work of Robert Jesse, a psychedelic strategist in Northern California and a founder of the Council on Spiritual Practices. Its purpose was to safely and effectively make "direct experience of the sacred more available to more people" and to "help individuals and spiritual communities bring the insights, grace, and joy that arise from direct perception of the divine into their daily lives."

Jesse, who studied engineering at Johns Hopkins, brought together Roland Griffiths, the principal investigator in the new Hopkins study of religious professional, and Bill Richards, who grew up in the Methodist church, studied at Yale Divinity School in the 1960s and remains active in an Episcopal parish. The author of the 2016 book *Sacred Knowledge—Psychedelics and Religious Experience*, Richards is the human link between the first and second waves of research and clinical practice into the healing power of entheogens.

For more than half a century, Richards has been working to

persuade both the theological establishment and the scientific community to seriously study the sacred dimensions of the psychedelic experience. In the early 1960s, as a young grad student fresh off his first LSD trip, he approached the head of the theology school at Yale. "He was worried that I'd lost my ability to think critically. He was more into Freudian theory and threatened by the idea of religious experience," Richards recalled. "But once you've glimpsed these states of consciousness, once you see the reality of the sacred, you don't forget it. You *know*."[12]

Fifty years later, some psychedelic researchers are pushing back against a mystical mindset that permeates this growing community of entheogenic explorers. Even that word, "entheogenic," which many have come to favor over "psychedelic," presumes that these plants, fungi and chemical compounds do, in fact, put us in touch with "the divine within." Richards has become something of a lightning rod among Jewish and secular scholars critical of the mystical and "New Age" predilections of the psychedelic therapy movement.

In his review of Richard's book *Sacred Knowledge*, DMT researcher Rick Strassman warns that the work at Johns Hopkins may alienate both the scientific community *and* the religious establishment. "Clinical research with psychedelics must remain within the mainstream," Strassman writes. "Overreaching into theology and religion, most obviously exemplified by the loose use of 'mystical' to describe particular drug effects, is certain to generate backlash from bona fide religions. No religious tradition is going to simply accept the proposition that their foundational spiritual experience is 'mystical consciousness' that most people can reach with several hours of psychotherapy and a psychedelic drug."[13]

Matthew Johnson, a professor of psychiatry and behavioral sciences at Johns Hopkins University in Baltimore, broke rank with Richards when he published a paper titled "Consciousness, Religion and Gurus: Pitfalls of Psychedelic Medicine." Johnson sees "danger" in "scientists and clinicians imposing their personal religious and spiritual beliefs on the practice of psychedelic medicine." He cites a pervasive "loosely held eclectic collection of various beliefs drawn piecemeal from mystical traditions, Eastern religions, and indigenous cultures, perhaps best described by the term 'new age.'"

Johnson was one of several secular-oriented researchers who published papers in 2021 in which they challenged the mystics in their midst.[14] "For whatever reason," Bill told me, "they just don't like religion. That's their right, but this is a rich realm of human experience…Mysticism is not beyond the scope of scientific enquiry. It is at the frontier of scientific enquiry."

Like the term "psychedelic," Richards said, "mystical experience" is becoming a term accepted by science. "Some prefer terms like 'non-dual,' or 'unitive,' or 'transcendental.' Choose your word, but this is coming into the mainstream of science."

"I've certainly had psychedelic experiences that are *not* sacred," Richards added. "I've had psychotic ones and psycho-dynamic ones. But I have had sacred experiences. I don't know if I had them or they had me, but I can't find a better word than 'sacred.'"[15]

Since the turn of the millennium, Bill Richards, Roland Griffiths, and Robert Jesse have collaborated on several Hopkins studies. One gave either psilocybin or a placebo to thirty-six "hallucinogenically naive adults." In the end, two-thirds of those who got the drug rated the psilocybin sessions as being "among the five most spiritually significant experiences of their lives." Another research project studied the effects that a psychedelic experience had on experienced meditation practitioners.

All that work led up to the current project conducted by researchers at both Johns Hopkins and NYU Langone Health titled "The Effects of Psilocybin-Facilitated Experience on the Psychology and Effectiveness of Religious Professionals." Twelve research subjects were recruited by Hopkins, and another twelve at NYU. "We hypothesize that religious professionals, given their interests, training, and life experience, will be able to make nuanced discriminations of their psilocybin experiences," the NYU study summary states. "A primary objective is to investigate changes in psychological functioning, spirituality, health, well-being, prosocial attitudes and behavior in professional religious leaders that may occur after receiving psilocybin under supportive conditions."

The study began in 2015. It has taken the organizers longer than expected to recruit volunteers, conduct the trials and write up their conclusions. As a journalist interested in exploring these realms, I played an indirect role in the recruitment of several of the subjects. Knowing my background as a reporter on the religion beat, Griffiths invited me to write an article on the study, which at that point had attracted only one ordained minister. Roland told me he hoped to see how a psychedelic experience would "an effect their engagement with their vocation."

"Clergy burnout is a very real and common phenomenon," he said. "They may feel burdened with administrative responsibility and may be losing some of the inspiration that brought them into ministry in the first place. What I would most hope to see is that this kind of experience would resonate with the reasons they were initially drawn into ministry and empower them to engage with their congregation in renewed and exciting ways."[16]

My article about the study, written for Religion News Service, appeared in a variety of newspapers and periodicals across the country, including the *Washington Post* and *Christian Century*. Hunt Priest, the Episcopal priest who volunteered for the study and later started a Christian psychedelic society, read my article in *Christian Century* and passed it along to his old friend from seminary, Roger Joslin. The third clergyman profiled in this chapter, the Lutheran James Lindberg, saw a later story that was prompted by my initial reporting.

It's not surprising that Griffiths and his research team had trouble finding subjects from the Roman Catholic Church, conservative Christian denominations and other faiths. Some religious traditions, including Muslims and Mormons, prohibit the use of alcohol and other intoxicants. Some Christian churches are also wary. The United Methodist Church, for example, states in its Book of Resolutions,"Psychedelics or hallucinogens, which include LSD, psilocybin, mescaline, PCP, and DMT, produce changes in perception and altered states of consciousness. Not only is medical use of psychedelics or hallucinogens limited, if present at all, but the use of these drugs may result in permanent psychiatric problems…Therefore, as The United Methodist Church: We oppose the use of all drugs, except in cases of appropriate medical supervision."

Seven years after my first story on the clergy study, when I began a new series of interviews for this book, the researchers at Hopkins and NYU had still not published their findings. But a lot happened in those seven years.

Media coverage of psychedelic-assisted therapy has played a key role in the mainstreaming of a movement that emerged from the underground, and first gained some respectability on the medical and academic fringe. In 2015, I published a series of articles in the *San Francisco Chronicle* and journalist Michael Pollan published a long piece in *The New Yorker*. In 2017, I came out with a book titled *Changing Our Minds—Psychedelic Sacraments and the New Psychotherapy*. A little more than a year later, Pollan published *How to Change Your Mind—What the New Science of Psychedelics Teaches Us About Consciousness, Dying, Addiction, Depression and Transcendence*. Pollan's book—like his popular works on food—jumped to the top of the *New York Times* bestseller list and stayed there for quite some time.

According to the National Survey on Drug Use and Health, 1.4 million Americans tried hallucinogens for the first time in 2020. This surging popularity was partly fueled by journalists reporting on the ongoing campaign to re-schedule and decriminalize psychedelics. More recently, there's been a shift toward more balanced coverage of the psychedelic revival, including stories about the potential psychological risks these drugs pose for some people.[17]

Media coverage of the seemingly miraculous cures of research subjects—often long before the actual results of a clinical trial are published—have been a key part of the psychedelic therapy crusade. MAPS, the Multidisciplinary Association for Psychedelic Studies, has long used this strategy in its effort to raise money, attract new volunteers and sway public opinion. MAPS has been working for some thirty years and has spent more than $30 million on its clinical trials designed to convince the U.S. Food and Drug Administration to reclassify MDMA so it can be routinely used to treat patients suffering from PostTraumatic Stress Disorder.

In May of 2015, I published a story on the front page of the *San Francisco Chronicle* about Nigel McCourry, a former lance corporal in the U.S. Marine Corps and an Iraqi war veteran, whose life was nearly destroyed by PTSD until he discovered the healing power of a drug known on the street as "Ecstasy." In May 2022, the *New York Times* ran its own version of the Nigel McCourry story. Yet, seven years later, the final results of this clinical trial have yet to be published and MDMA officially remains a Schedule 1 drug, meaning in the eyes of the federal government it is easily abused and has no medical value.

In my opinion, MAPS is right and the FDA is wrong. I no longer pretend to be "objective" in my reporting about the potential therapeutic and spiritual benefits of psychedelic drugs. But I also worry that much of the media coverage over the past decade—including some of my own—has led to unrealistic expectations that MDMA or psilocybin are the latest in a long time of "miracle drugs." Psychedelics put the user in a highly suggestible state of mind—whether they are taken at raves or in controlled research settings. What one thinks will happen is often (but not always) what does happen. It's very hard to separate the hype from the science.

In my latest interview with Roland Griffiths, this veteran scientist bristled at the suggestion that there is any theological and political agenda behind the research at Johns Hopkins. "Although this is not about changing culture, it has implications for cultural change, but we were not trying to turn people into evangelical psychedelic proponents. I don't think any of the investigators wanted that," Roland told me. "We are in a disconcerting psychedelic bubble right now in which people have unbridled enthusiasm for the potential of psychedelics to cure everything. They minimize the risks and make it sound like psychedelics are completely harmless. Psychedelics are not harmless. People are going to die. People are going to become psychotic. We are in a bubble and that bubble is going to break. We need to get realistic as to what this program is about.

"I'm trained as a scientist. I'm a skeptic. Going into the first study I had doubts about the outcome. I thought some psychedelic enthusiasts were unrealistic about some of the claims they made. But my initial thoughts were changed by the data. And the data were so astounding and so different than anything I'd seen in behavioral pharmacology of mood-altering drugs that it became a point of fascination for me. That first study was preceded by my involvement with meditation, which continues. But I didn't come in with an agenda." [18]

Two ghostly figures swirl between the lines of Matthew Johnson's critique of the "New Age" mysticism that underlies so much of today's psychedelic movement. Timothy Leary died in 1996. Richard Alpert, known for more than half his life as Ram Dass, passed in 2019. Yet the posthumous presence of Leary and Alpert can still be felt in Johnson's critique, in Bill Richards defense of the sacred, and in Roland Griffiths' insistence that the researchers at Hopkins and NYU are simply "following the data."

So let's end this chapter by going back to the scene of the crime—to Harvard University, the school that kicked out the dynamic duo from the halls of academia sixty years ago.

Alpert, an assistant professor in psychology, was fired in the spring of 1963 for violating university regulations and tripping with undergraduates outside of his formal research project. Leary, a lecturer on a three-year Harvard contract, was let go after abandoning his Harvard classroom and heading down to Mexico to start a psychedelic retreat center. Their "Harvard drug scandal," fueled by rumors of heterosexual and homosexual impropriety, wound up on the front page of the *New York Times* and across the glossy centerfolds of *Life* magazine. Leary, a trickster and provocateur, went on to position himself as the high priest of the psychedelic counterculture, winding up in prison. Alpert, a lifelong spiritual seeker, travelled to India, met a guru, and returned in his Ram Dass incarnation, preaching his charismatic mix of Jewish humor, psychedelic insight, and Hindu piety.

As mentioned earlier, it's too easy to blame Leary and Alpert for the Nixon administration's broader war on the 1960s counterculture in all its flowerings—political, social, and psychedelic. But those infamous Harvard profs most certainly *helped* set back scientific and scholarly study of psychedelic drugs for some three decades.

Harvard has long been emblematic of America's Protestant religious establishment, serving as an intellectual beacon to all those mainline churches that have in recent decades been shunted to the sidelines of the nation's increasingly eclectic spiritual life. Harvard was established by the Puritans in 1636 as a "church in the wilderness" and training ground for clergymen in the newly established Massachusetts Bay Colony.

Compared to Johns Hopkins or NYU, this academic institution has been relatively slow to embrace the new wave of medical and scientific research into psychedelic-assisted therapy. But that is starting to change in, of all places, Harvard Divinity School and one of its academic units, the Center for the Study of World Religions. It's there that I ran into Rachael Petersen, a young woman whose story shows how psilocybin-assisted therapy can inspire a new generation of psychedelic scholar/strategists.

Petersen was born in 1989 in Temple, Texas, a town on Interstate 35 about halfway between Waco, infamous for the Branch Davidian religious cult, and Austin, a city dedicated to keeping it weird. She went off to college at Rice University in nearby Houston, earning an undergraduate degree in anthropology and environmental policy. But much of Petersen's young life had been defined by the demon of depression, a story she told with poetic clarity at a Harvard seminar on "psychedelics and the future of religion."

"Perhaps it began around age twelve, as I lie on the floor crying for days, watching Texas thunderstorms come and go through closed blinds, feeling nothing at all," she recalled. "Or when my thoughts suddenly stopped the dance of the world with their stuckness. Or when good things began to roll off my back like water, but the bad gathered in my pockets like heavy stones. Of course, the doctors assured my parents that depression was not a crisis. It was an equation, and medications would balance my brain. Combinations were tested, and doses increased, and therapy marked the passing of years. And I managed periods of success and joy, even, but no SSRI or psychoanalysis managed to touch what I describe as a deeper substrate of despair."

In 2017, Rachael was studying climate change and environmental destruction as a policy consultant for the World Resources Institute, the National Geographic Society, and other large foundations. She was also struggling with depression, which inspired her to enroll in one of the clinical trials at Johns Hopkins. "I joke that it was a bait and switch," she told me. "I went in hoping that they'd cure my depression, but came out with an entirely new worldview."

"It was an ontological ass-kicking. I didn't believe in any sort of metaphysical realm beyond what we can see or perceive. I was a joyless, materialist, atheist before the trial. Now I'm in divinity school. I had something of a conversion experience. Now I hold sadness and despair very differently than I did before the trial. The trial worked, but not in a straight pharmacological way. It's not like they just tweaked something in my brain. Now I live in a totally different reality.

"I was working in climate policy, and I guess I underestimated how depressing that work is. It's futile. I was burned out. That was the water I swan in. I know it's a cliche, but I had this experience (with psilocybin) of becoming one with nature. Then going through this horrible apocalyptic montage. I became Earth and then it occurred to me that Earth was being destroyed...What do I do with this? How does one live? The minute I asked that, my experience broke open into this encounter with nothingness. Not a scary nothingness, but an abiding nothingness. Like there was something before this. There will be something after this. It was like a new frame."

Several years later, Petersen spoke at that previously cited Harvard seminar, which was part of a year-long series at the divinity school. In her talk, she connected her sickness and its cure. "There's common wisdom in the psychedelic community that these experiences are ineffable. But I find despair to be just as challenging to grasp, and as profound and mysterious. There's a dark kind of gnosis to it, an authority with which it forecloses on all possibility other than itself."

Her reflections on her experiences in the Hopkins depression study inspired Petersen to study theology. She became a visiting fellow at the Harvard Divinity School's Center for the Study of World Religions and signed on as the psychedelics and religion program director at the Riverstyx Foundation, started by the philanthropist and psychedelic therapy advocate T. Cody Swift. The foundation is one of the Johns Hopkins' funders. When we last spoke, Petersen was working with Roland Griffiths, William Richards and others to help write up the findings of their study of clergy who came to their Baltimore lab for a psychedelic baptism.

"There's such poor literacy around religion," she said. "I do sometimes worry that the psychedelic movement is cashing in with collective glee on the failing of religion. 'Religion is dying. It's not giving people what they need. We're going to give them what they need.' There's almost a patronizing quality to that. Some in the psychedelic community have this premise that religion has lost touch with its true purpose and its true purpose is to connect people with the transcendent. But that's not what modern religion thinks its role is. It is teaching people how to live in an ethical way. Community is something it cares about. You can get those things without touching the divine. Sometimes the divine has very little to do with morality."[19]

Nevertheless, she agrees mainstream religion can learn something from the mystical encounters experienced by the religious professionals at Hopkins and NYU.

"We've lost touch with how to connect to primary religious experience," Petersen said. "Modern traditions, especially the Abrahamic traditions, are spooked by it. Christianity has burned people at the stake and killed off indigenous traditions for saying (psychoactive) plants can show us another realm of being. It goes deep."

Petersen delivered her Harvard presentation over the Internet—during one of the more deadly surges of COVID virus. She called on the psychedelic therapy movement to broaden the conversation beyond what's happening in our brains and start paying more attention to what's happening in society. "It feels remiss not to mention the moment we're in," she said. "Rates of anxiety, suicide, and depression have spiked under the pandemic. And even before then, Americans were walking on a tightrope. We live in a society where we believe people don't deserve access to health care, where you have to work your butt off to make a living wage, where people don't have affordable family care.

"The most important thing we can do for mental health is fix our society, and not propagate the psychedelic narrative that your suffering begins and ends in your brain. But regardless of that, these medicines are going to be legalized. So questions about equity should be paramount. My worst nightmare is that not only will we not fix society, but these will become expensive boutique drugs for people who can afford them."

ONE OF THE more interesting organizations to emerge out of the Hopkins/NYU sessions with religious professionals is Ligare, the Christian psychedelic society founded by Hunt Priest. In the spring of 2022, Ligare held its first psychedelic retreat in the Netherlands, where psilocybin is legal in the form of "truffles."

Priest described this first gathering at a facility outside Amsterdam as "a typical Christian retreat with a regular pattern of prayer, shared meals, Bible study, walks in the woods, and time to be together." All of those on retreat were mainline Protestant clergy, including pastors, chaplains and spiritual directors. Two were from Canada, and the rest lived in the U.S. On the third day, the thirteen participants, overseen by six guides, took magic mushrooms.

"All of these people were prepared spiritually as Christians, and I think they made meaning of the experience through a Christian lens," Priest told me. "But that doesn't mean we all have to have a walk with Jesus...No one had what I would say was a strictly 'Christian' experience, and no one had an experience that was antithetical to Christianity.

"We gave people a day and a half to begin to make meaning, to share their experiences after they 'came back down from the mountaintop.' We began to figure out ways to integrate their experience—not just the truffles, but the whole retreat experience—into their ministry and into their day-to-day lives. In some ways, it was a very normal Christian retreat, except there was this big experience with psilocybin truffles halfway through it."

In 2023, Oregon became the first state in the U.S. to legalize and regulate the facilitated use of magic mushrooms. So, in a year or two, Priest hopes that "we can have a five-day retreat at a church camp in Oregon."

This Episcopal priest acknowledges that psychedelics may challenge our preconceived ideas about God. But that, he said, is a good thing. "We want to be careful about making God small. I don't think the intent of Christianity is to put God in a small box. I don't think that's what Jesus was about. Jesus was about putting God in a more expansive, cosmological place. You especially see this in the Gospel of John, where Christ is cosmic. That's a very mystical telling of the Jesus story in John's gospel. Some see real connections between that and their own psychedelic experiences."[20]

Priest doesn't see psychedelics as a way to stem the tide of Christians leaving the fold. "This is not a marketing technique. It's an invitation to the church to meet people where they are, to not be so concerned about institutional maintenance or institutional growth, but to take seriously our call to be present to people, and to their own healing, and their own spiritual life. We can find places for people who are interested in psychedelics and make room for them to bring their stories and their experience into our communities and to inform the Christian community. If the church is not interested in healing and the transformation of people, and culture, and civilization, then I'm not sure *what* we're doing."

CHAPTER 2
ON BEING PSYCHEDELIC AND JEWISH

Judaism and Christianity each have centuries-old mystical paths. But since the 1960s, and in the current psychedelic revival, countless North American psychonauts have turned to Buddhism, Hinduism or shamanism to understand their sudden connection to divine reality.

We'll hear in the next two chapters from two scholars—Rabbi Art Green and the Rev. John Mabry—both of whom have thought deeply and written extensively about Jewish and Christian mysticism.

How do they view a spiritual revival fueled by psychedelic drugs and sacred plant medicines? Will these revelatory glimpses of transcendence, unitive awareness, and divine love inspire seekers to take another look at the mystical traditions hidden within their ancestral faiths?

But before turning to the rabbi and the reverend, let's first consider a more familiar name in the pantheon of psychedelic spiritualists.

That would be the aforementioned Richard Alpert, the Jewish psychology professor fired from his post at Harvard

University in 1963. The following year Alpert co-authored *The Psychedelic Experience* with Harvard colleagues Timothy Leary and Ralph Metzner, an influential tripping guidebook based on the Buddhist theology of *The Tibetan Book of the Dead*. In the late 1960s, Alpert went on his celebrated pilgrimage to India, became the disciple of a Hindu guru, and took the name Ram Dass.

Alpert was a master of one-liners, including the quip, "I'm only Jewish on my parents side."

Leary and Alpert were encouraged to interpret their psychedelic experience through Eastern mysticism by two earlier psychedelic pioneers, the British writer Aldous Huxley, and his friend and mentor Gerald Heard, an Anglo-Irish philosopher and mystic. Heard and Huxley were deeply influenced by two modern Indian spiritual movements—Vedanta and Theosophy, along with the spiritualist writings of William James, the "father of American psychology."

It's no secret that psychedelics often inspire profound mystical experiences, even among people who previously considered themselves atheists or long ago fell away from organized religion. These plants, fungi and chemical compounds have the power to deconstruct our preconceived ideas about the nature of reality and how we relate to ourselves and the world around us.

Mystical experiences—whether occasioned by psychedelics or some other path—often lead the spiritual seeker away from religious orthodoxy. This is why some Christian theologians warn that *myst-i-cism* "begins with mist, puts the I in the center, and ends in schism." Psychedelics can spark blessed connectedness, but they can also fuel grandiosity, paranoia and existential dread. It may be wise to recall an old Jewish tale from the first century about four rabbis who saw the face of God. One died, another went crazy, the third became a heretic, and only the fourth "entered in peace and departed in peace."[1]

One of the key Jewish-born messiahs of the psychedelic religion that emerged in the 1960s and 1970s was the aforementioned Ram Dass. His journey to the East and devotion to his guru, Neem Karoli Baba, inspired the 1971 hippie classic, *Be Here Now*, and decades of service lived according to the spiritual teachings of bhakti yoga. Ram Dass encouraged a significant cohort of the acid subculture to go beyond the ephemera of psychedelic insight to pursue meditation and other kinder, gentler forms of mind expansion. At the same time, he became the poster child for turning your back on the faith of your forefathers.

Like millions of other Jewish Americans, Ram Dass' ancestors emigrated to the United States from Russia and Eastern Europe around the turn of the twentieth century. They came in search of economic opportunity and to escape various forms of anti-Semitism, some of it deadly. His Judaism, like that of so many others, was more social than spiritual.

Most of this man's references to Judaism in his talks and writings, both as Richard Alpert and as Ram Dass, are laced with sarcasm and self-deprecating humor. "Until you know a good middle-class Jew, upwardly mobile, anxiety-ridden, and neurotic, you haven't met a real achiever!" he writes in *Be Here Now*. Judaism, he said a couple years later, is for "people who in one lifetime are not going to begin to awaken." Jews, he said, "aren't primarily interested in what happened to Moses up in the Mountain. Their primary interest is what he brought back."

As a journalist on the religion beat, I interviewed Ram Dass a half-dozen times over a span of more than two decades. Our final encounters were a long series of conversations in 2008, over the course of three days at his home on Maui, when I was doing research for my book, *The Harvard Psychedelic Club*. His

Jewish heritage rarely came up during those interviews. I didn't press him on it, and he didn't seem to want to go beyond his great one-liners about Jewish angst, such as, "If you think you're enlightened, go and spend a week with your parents."

Ira Rifkin, one of my friends and colleagues on the religion beat, did have an extended conversation with Ram Dass about his Jewish heritage. It was in the early 1990s. Ram Dass had just turned sixty and had been invited to give a lecture on "Judaism and Spirituality" at a Jewish college in Los Angeles. He crammed like he was preparing for a college exam, reading the Torah and studying the works of Jewish scholars like Abraham Joshua Heschel, Martin Buber and Adin Steinsaltz.

"I started to get into what it would feel like to be a very religious Orthodox Jew. I began to see the heartfelt beauty of being a person who truly loves God in a Jewish way, how it related to lineage and community, how the mitzvah (life guidelines under Jewish law) are all requirements for remembering God," Ram Dass told Ira. "My belief is that I wasn't born into Judaism by accident, and so I need to find ways to honor that."[2]

In his talk at the University of Judaism, Ram Dass confessed that both he and his father, a successful Boston lawyer and Jewish philanthropist, believed that the best way to assimilate into American life was "learning how to be ashamed of their parents...Can you feel the pain of all that?"

"During my time of growing up, we started out as Orthodox and became liberal Conservative," he said. "The pain for my father and mother was that they went through that transition. I never knew the other end. They went through knowing what the laws were and then choosing not to follow them." By the time he came of age, "nobody cared that I be religious. They just cared that I be a Jew." Ram Dass confessed in his talk that it saddened him to be accused of having "led more people away from Judaism than anybody else."

"It was not, certainly, my intention to lead people from Judaism," he said. "I was responding to the truth of my own heart."

In the end, Ram Dass never really embraced his Judaism. He remained devoted to his guru and committed to a universalist philosophy centered around Hinduism and Buddhism. But he admitted that "had I been in a warm relationship with Judaism, it may well have been that I would have found—through the Kabbalah, the Zohar, the Book of Brilliance—the maps that would have given me some structure to what I had experienced" on psychedelics.[3]

Toward the end of my research for this book I stumbled across the transcript of an interview I did with Ram Dass on March 2, 1993—nearly thirty years ago. I'd been cleaning out old newspaper files as part of a major decluttering and must confess that I had completely forgotten this particular conversation.

Back in the 1960s, Ram Dass said in that interview, "churches had the forms and the rituals. Younger people came to get the spirit and only got calcified ideas and a patriarchal, vertical religion. In Judaism, most rabbis had never had a spiritual experience."

Through psychedelics and meditative practices, he said, many Jewish baby boomers "went off into the spiritual dimensions of their own experience." In the 1990s, he added, some of those seekers were starting to return via the Hassidic mystical wing of Judaism to find a "more intimate relationship with God."

"If you go deep enough into the mystical tradition," Ram Dass said, "it feels like you are reading a Buddhist text."

Four years after this interview, Ram Dass suffered a major

stroke that left him partially paralyzed and severely limited his ability to speak. He died in his home on Maui in late 2019 at the age of eighty-eight. In our 1993 interview, Ram Dass specifically mentioned the work of Rabbi Art Green and his "far out" books exploring Jewish spirituality.

RABBI ART GREEN'S first acid trip unfolded in 1965, just as the psychedelic revolution was gathering steam. His cosmic vehicle was an LSD-laced sugar cube offered up in Cambridge, Massachusetts by a band of pioneering psychonauts brought together by the Catholic-born Leary and the Jewish-bred Alpert.

At the time, Green was taking a short break from his studies as a rabbinical student at the Jewish Theological Seminary, sitting alongside a lake in western Massachusetts. He now recalls his psychedelic baptism as "mind-blowing and gentle at the same time."

"I understood that there was level after level after level and mind after mind after mind. You could open it up and open it up ad infinitum. That's what the mystics had been talking about. It was very clear to me. They talk about God as the *ein sof*, the endless. I saw this endless continuum between the ordinary human mind and the cosmic mind."[4]

Green estimated that he took LSD seven or eight times back in the 1960s and 1970s, and guided LSD trips for another ten to twenty friends. "I almost got kicked out of rabbinical school when someone heard that I was guiding trips in my dorm room," he recalled. "I somehow covered my ass and got the award for outstanding senior student."

Since then, the aging rabbi has watched as countless Christians and Jews in the U.S.—both in the 1960s and in the recent psychedelic revival—turned toward Eastern mysticism or Native American shamanism. In his view, this rejection of their Jewish and Christian traditions is "one of the great tragedies of this whole period."

"Judaism and Christianity had become very domesticated in the West, dressed in very rational and somewhat superficial garb," he told me. "In the 1960s, a lot of the psychedelic revolution was wrapped up in adolescent rebellion. It was a rejection of 1950s bourgeois complacency. Since the religion of your bar mitzvah or your confirmation in church had been the religion of that bourgeois complacency, you wanted to choose something entirely different.

"Plus, those traditions were very much centered on a personal God figure. The psychedelic experience doesn't necessarily lead one to that. It can, depending on what you go into it with, but it doesn't necessarily lead there. If you're an atheist you want to go to a Buddhist spirituality that doesn't make you believe in God."

Rabbi Green went on to establish a countercultural Jewish community in the Boston area that sought to renew and revive this ancient faith. He has spent most of his eight decades on the planet studying the Zohar, the thirteenth-century classic of medieval Kabbalah, along with the eighteenth-century Eastern Europe teachings of Hasidic rabbis. He is the author of numerous books on Jewish mysticism, including *Radical Judaism: Rethinking God and Tradition*.

Rabbi Green was born in Newark, New Jersey in 1941, ten years after Alpert. But unlike Alpert, Green had Jewish maps by which to navigate and understand the psychedelic experience. He was also close friends with Rabbi Zalman Schachter-Shalomi, one of the leaders of the mystical Jewish Renewal movement of the late 1960s and early 1970s. Reb Zalman, as he was known, strayed further from Orthodox Judaism than

Green. "We both did acid and mushrooms," Green recalled, "but Zalman became a real believer in the New Age.... Everybody was going to take LSD and that was going to change the world. Clergy should become LSD practitioners and give it to their congregation, which will change people's consciousness. A spiritual rebirth was about to happen. That's what the Age of Aquarius was all about.

"I was younger and I saw too many people I knew who were tripping and listening to rock music all night and going crazy, or who were tripping and going out on the town. Then there were the followers of (cult leader Charles) Manson, tripping and going out and killing people. I felt psychedelics were a wonderful tool, but very easily misused, and I did not think the New Age was coming. Zalman was a messianic Jew, and by that I don't mean a Hebrew Christian (as in the 'Jews for Jesus' movement). I mean someone who believes redemption is right around the corner.

"I'm a person who believes that the wicked Kingdom of Rome is here to stay. We are going to live in the shadow of evil for a long time and have to create little pockets of light so the light will survive amongst the evil forces around us."

Nevertheless, Green still believes that the cautious use of psychedelics can open one up to the same higher states of consciousness that are described by Jewish mystics. "There is a chemical component to what we call mystical experience. If that happens in the brain with psychedelics, I don't see anything inauthentic about that. The problem is that if someone has that experience after twenty years of meditation, there's a certain gravitas to that experience. If you pop a pill and have that experience you don't understand what happened or have that gravitas. You don't have the tools to approach it, to integrate it into your life. But that doesn't make the experience itself inauthentic. It means that the context in which it takes place is a less serious context."

Green has been thinking and writing about Jewish mysticism and psychoactive drugs for more than half a century. In 1968, he anonymously published (under the name Itzik Lodzer) an article titled "Notes from the Jewish Underground: Psychedelics and Kabbalah." During a video interview over the Internet, Green explained what he meant in that essay when he said psychedelics allow us to see the world "from God's point of view." He was in Jerusalem, and I was home on an island in the San Francisco Bay.

"I am, theologically, a monist," Green replied. "There is only one ultimate reality. There isn't God, and the world and God and the self. There is one ultimate reality, and we are part of it. Each of us is here for a tiny flick in evolutionary time. We do what we do, but we are all part of this greater process. We see the world, of course, from the point of view of our own individual self, but there is a way to get into the mind of that One, since we are all part of that One, into the mind of that One. In psychedelic experience there is a way to see the world from the mind of that One. We see it from above or within. I prefer the internal metaphor to the vertical metaphor. Western religion is very oriented toward the vertical metaphor. God is 'up there.' God is up there and we are down here. I prefer the internal metaphor. The One is in there and we are the outer manifestation."

I mentioned that perhaps that's what Jesus was talking about when, according to the Bible, he says, "The Kingdom of Heaven is within you." Yes, the rabbi replied, or as the Jews would say, "Make for me a tabernacle and I will dwell within you."

Sam Shonkoff, a professor of Jewish studies at the Graduate Theological Union in Berkeley, said Jewish psychonauts coming of age in the generations following the baby boomers struggle with many of the same issues as those in the 1960s and 1970s.

"Like the previous movements, the current generation continues to grapple with modern disenchantment," he told me. "And like the baby boomers, I suspect that psychedelics will again play a significant role. Jewish mystical states and techniques of past centuries are so foreign to today's secularized Jewish souls, and it seems that many are once again turning to psychedelics as a sort of jump start for inert engines."

Shonkoff, who studies modern Jewish renewal movements and works with the UC Berkeley Center for the Science of Psychedelics, said there is one big difference between today's psychedelic scene and the situation half a century ago.

"Psychedelics are so much more mainstream and increasingly aligned with 'the establishment' than they were in the sixties," he said. "On one hand, this could open up potent possibilities for contemporary Jewish renewal. On the other hand, it could devolve into a sort of conformist trend that slips into the soulless snares of capitalism and big pharma. A major question for Jewish psychedelia today is how to tap into the creative forces of psychoactive plants and fungi without losing sight of the distinct gravity of ancestral Jewish sources."

My Zoom interview with Art Green reminded me of a memorable encounter I had in Jerusalem many years ago with Rabbi Adin Steinsaltz, the noted Torah scholar. There have been many times in my life when I've felt Jewish, especially when hanging out with Jewish friends, connecting with that sardonic, world-weary wisdom that feels so right. Walking into this Orthodox rabbi's book-lined study was one of those moments. Actually, the feeling began even before I reached his office, when I was walking through the streets of the Jewish Quarter in the old city.

My encounter with Rabbi Steinsaltz happened in the spring of 1986. I was in the Middle East, reporting for a series of articles for the *San Francisco Examiner*. Tensions between the Israelis and the Palestinians were, once again, rising and would soon erupt into the first intifada, or uprising, in Gaza and the West Bank. One of my Jewish friends had recommended that I interview Steinsaltz, an authority on the kabbalah, the ancient Jewish mystical teachings that were finding a new audience among the spiritual seekers of my generation.

Something hit me when I walked into the rabbi's office. Perhaps it was only the random movement of cumulus clouds, but the sunlight seemed to pour into this room on cue. The bearded, bespectacled sage leaned back in his chair and another burst of light illuminated the arching white walls of his office.[5]

Steinsaltz, then a frail five foot six, with sparkling eyes and elfin charm, was born in Israel in 1937 to Zionist settlers from eastern Europe. He read Marx before he ever opened the Torah. But at fifteen, he shocked his family and friends by enrolling in a yeshiva, a traditional school of Orthodox Judaism. "In my generation," he told me, "that was something people wouldn't even think of as a remote possibility. You could do whatever you wanted—become a Communist or leave the country. But a return to religion was beyond madness. It was unthinkable." So what led him to that path? "I'm by nature a skeptic," he replied. "Skepticism is the ability to look at things for truth, not just accepting them. I'm not a believer, so I ceased believing in atheism."

Then the rabbi turned the tables. "Are you an atheist," he asked me, "or a believer?"

"Neither," I said. "My mother is Jewish, so I guess I'm

Jewish. My father was Protestant, so I'm a baptized Christian. If you want to know which religious philosophy seems, to me, like the truth, I'd have to say it's somewhere between Buddhism and Taoism."

"You know," the rabbi replied. "Judaism is usually depicted as a purely Western religion, but that's just not true. We are a mixture of East and West. Many of our basic notions are from the East."

Many Jews and Christians, Steinsaltz told me, have a superficial understanding of the human potential involved in living according to the commandments of the Bible—such as honoring the shabbat, or sabbath. This is not about archaic prohibitions, he said, but a time for turning inward, for meditation—or perhaps, I might add, for considering whatever insights one might have on a psychedelic journey.

"Unless you understand shabbat, all you see is that people don't want you to drive. They don't want you to enjoy yourself. That's one of the reasons shabbat was never successful as a Christian experiment, even though it was imitated by the Puritans, sometimes very strictly. But it was an outward experience. It was just a prohibition and became a really oppressive thing. For most Jews, shabbat is really enjoyable. It's the joy of *not* doing things. In a way the whole notion of shabbat is that it's a reversal. Normally, one's basic drive is outward. You are changing things. On shabbat, you allow things to change you."

Jewish mysticism begins with a mind-blowing book purportedly written by the Prophet Ezekiel between the years 593-571 B.C.E., when the Jews were living in exile in Babylon. "Then I looked, and behold, a whirlwind was coming out of the north, a great cloud with raging fire engulfing itself, and a brightness was all around it and radiating out of its midst like the color of amber," the prophet reports. Ezekiel goes on to describe visions of a creature with four wings and four faces, each face half man and half beast. Alongside this fantastical creature was a wheel with rims that "were so high they were awesome, and the rims were full of eyes..."

Yes, it reads a bit like a trip report from the Haight-Ashbury, circa 1967.

How does Rabbi Green explain all this? And how does he think Jewish spiritual tradition can inform the psychedelic exploration and help practitioners integrate that experience into their daily lives?

There's a long pause as the rabbi closes his eyes and gently rocks his head up and down. "The Jewish mystical tradition has existed for a couple thousand years," he replied. "There's great variety in it. There is not one teaching or method...We have ancient texts, going back to the second, third and fourth century about people who ascended to the heavens, through the seven heavens, and they meet angels on the way and have various conversations along the way, and they finally come to the seventh heaven and they praise God and sing in the angelic chorus. The chorus that surrounds the throne of the One."

"Those texts are clearly about experiences that some people had. Psychedelics help you understand that those texts are about something real. They are not just fantasy texts, but some kind of real experience, whether the person who wrote the text had the experience or was just in the tradition of the experience. They didn't, literally, go up in the sky, but there was an experience within them. Later, the Hasidic masters have a way of reading the whole Jewish tradition—all the rituals, all the observances, all the legal formula, as a means of achieving a oneness with God, or entry into the divine self. Psychedelics can be a push off the platform into those experiences. How can you integrate those experiences into your life? The experience is not difficult, but bringing it back into reality is what it's all about. The Jewish tradition is rich in ritual. But we need to get over worrying about doing it right, the compulsiveness, and use ritual forms as a stable entry into the upper universe. Then they can work beautifully. There's a re-entry phase. The personality has to be built again... a rebirthing process can happen. And having a spiritual guidebook from your tradition, whether it's Judaism or Christianity, can help immensely."

Green hopes that Jewish seekers will try to find a place for their faith in the psychedelic renaissance. "We want to preserve our path. Jews have been a minority for so long. The sense of self-preservation is just deeply ingrained in Jews. We don't want to see Judaism swept into a kind of neo-Christian universalist perennialism."

The rabbi hasn't tripped since the 1970s. Is he ready to try it again? "My friends here in Jerusalem are trying to convince me to do mushrooms with them. I probably will, because it seems to be coming up again as an issue. I'm eighty years old and I'm thinking about it. Why not?"

ANOTHER JEWISH PERSPECTIVE on all this comes from DMT researcher Rick Strassman, who argues that many of today's psychedelic scientists and other psychonauts are biased toward a "unitive-mystical" model that is more in line with Eastern mystical traditions like Buddhism or Hinduism. They downplay the "interactive-relational" model that may be more reflective of Jewish or Christian mysticism.

Strassman no longer believes in "neurotheology," at least if that is defined to mean that psychedelics cause feelings or hallucinations that we interpret as spiritually significant. He now puts God first, as in "theoneurology." This God, the Jewish creator God of the Hebrew scriptures, "constituted our mind-brain complex so that we can communicate with the spirit world."

Strassman—who was raised as a Jew but as a young man became a serious student of Zen Buddhism—told me in an interview some years ago that he was disinvited to conferences and talks because his more recent monotheistic ideas "were 'too religious' whereas ideas somehow Buddhism, Hinduism and shamanism were not."

In our most recent exchange, Rick continued to question whether the Jewish faith can be easily reconciled with "psychedelic religion of mystical consciousness."

"If one wishes to increase their commitment to and understanding of their ancestral faith, the first requirement is to learn about that faith through study, practice, and acquiring good teachers. If you wish your psychedelic experiences to be more spiritual, you need to be a more spiritual person. The notion that a highly emotional but cognitively meager mystical-unitive spiritual experience—one that is absent the normal senses of self, time, and space—underlies all major religious traditions is false. There are no such experiences recounted in the entire Hebrew Bible, the foundational text of Judaism, and which Christianity uses to support its claim of Jesus's messiahship. Instead, the fundamental spiritual experience in the Hebrew Bible is one of relationship and interaction, full of verbal exchange, between humans and God or God's angels."

Strassman, whose books include *DMT and the Soul of Prophecy*, said "any attempt to argue that Judaism's essential spiritual experience is mystical-unitive is an attempt to neutralize the distinguishing characteristic teachings of Judaism."

"Those teachings are the existence of one God, the Golden Rule, and the role of the Jewish people in history. This does not mean that Jews cannot trip, nor engage with the larger psychedelic community. However, it does mean that to remain true to their religion, Jews need to recognize that their religion stands outside of the psychedelic religion of mystical consciousness."[6]

Zac Kamenetz was born in Southern California in 1981, moving with his family to North Carolina before he started high school. They attended services in Reform movement synagogues. There was Hebrew school, a bar mitzvah, but "no talk of the divine or the spirit or anything." When he was in high school, Zac's parents insisted that he go on a two-month study tour to Israel. "I had a horrible time the first month. I didn't want to be there. I had a girlfriend back home. I was smoking weed. I was playing the lead in plays."

Then one day in the Holy Land, during a visit to an archeological site, the teenager had "a major unexplained, unrehearsed mystical experience." No psychedelics were involved. "Time stopped. Mind opened. A feeling of electricity and a divine presence. I was a religious person after that moment."

In 2012, after earning a master's degree in Biblical literature and languages from UC Berkeley and the adjacent Graduate Theological Union, Kamenetz was ordained as a rabbi. Four years later, he was working as an educator at the Jewish Community Center in San Francisco when he heard about Roland Griffith's research study at Johns Hopkins. Researchers there were offering psilocybin—the active ingredient in magic mushrooms—to religious professionals who had never had a psychedelic experience. "I may have chewed on a mushroom stem one summer, but I'd never had a psychedelic experience," Kamenetz said. "I didn't know what that was. I was a curious person. What is this? What is possible?"[7]

His wife had just given birth. She had reservations, but Kamenetz flew to Baltimore for his first trip in the spring of 2017. It was "powerful and positive," inspiring "a little more pep in my step." On the eve of his second trip, three months later, Kamenetz expected more beauty and gratitude. Instead, he just "felt like I'd been dropped into a deep, dark hole." It was a bit like the Rev. Rita Powell's experience of the void, chronicled in the previous chapter, but with a twist. "There was no fear," Zac recalled. "Just boredom."

Over the following months, Kamenetz began to research the foundations of the research protocols in the Hopkins study —everything from the music played during the sessions to the questionnaires designed to measure and quantify something as slippery as a mystical experience. Questions arose about the nature of the interventions in psychedelic research and psychedelic assisted therapy.

Psychedelics have the power to put people into vulnerable states of suggestibility. Kamenetz began to ask himself "how much of the experience is authentically mine and how much of it was influenced by what was being presented to me in the protocol." Was it his own mystical experience, or a type of revelation favored by the designers of the project?

"I have concerns for the spiritual and cultural health and wellbeing of my community," Kamenetz said. "What are the cultural assumptions about the meaning of my experience?... My assumptions about consciousness, reality and the nature of my soul are determined by my own tradition, orthodox Judaism, and may be different from the assumptions of any researcher or therapist who is creating the container for a psychedelic experience."

Those concerns led Kamenetz to found Shefa, an organization dedicated to Jewish psychedelic support, and to found the Jewish Psychedelic Summit with Natalie Ginsberg and

Madison Margolin in the spring of 2021. Shefa holds bimonthly integration circles where Jews from around the world can share and process their psychedelic experiences in a culturally and religiously sensitive setting.

To Rabbi Kamenetz, the narrowing of what constitutes a mystical experience in psychedelic discourse "leaves out the wide-ranging diversity of Jewish mystical experience and the diversity of mystical experience in other religious lineages and traditions."

"Right now, there is a culture of very active and very enthusiastic psychedelic Jews who are starting to wake up to the problem of cultural appropriation," said Kamenetz. "How can we authentically bridge our religious traditions and psychedelic states to mutually inform, enrich and re-enchant spiritual life?"

Organizations like Shefa fascinate Shonkoff, the Jewish studies professor. "What is all this psychedelic exploration going to do to these religious traditions. It's not going to leave them untouched. We are in a transitional moment in the unfolding of these religious traditions."

Shonkoff has studied the late 20th century neo-Hasidic movement. He, too, has concerns about the preconceptions of some of the researchers at Johns Hopkins and elsewhere. "For me, the whole idea that what these substances do is catalyze spiritual experiences is a culturally specific understanding of what these things are. It's rooted in a Protestant understanding of religion."

"Whatever they are doing at the Hopkins lab is clearly working for a lot of people in terms of having extraordinary, meaningful and in some ways healing, life-changing experiences," he said. "Where we get into trouble is where we fail to recognize that what they are doing is a tradition itself. It has its own history, its own places of reverence, and its own selection bias."[8]

Griffiths, the principal investigator in the Johns Hopkins study of religious professionals, was troubled by the allegation that his team was subtly leading its subjects into an amorphous New Age spirituality. "Most of our research on psychedelics and the primary mystical experience have been completely secularized, except perhaps for the word 'sacredness.' However, there's a secular equivalent to that word, which is the phrase "preciousness beyond belief." We are not introducing specific religious beliefs. We generally assess mystical experiences in a single questionnaire among many other questionnaires. We are evaluating as best we can the impact on how people think of their own religious traditions, how they think about their own ministry. Have their thoughts changed about that? But I do not believe that the study design is biased about outcome. I would be disappointed if some believe that there was a bias toward any religious tradition in the study. I don't think it's there. We tried to have symbols appropriate to all religious traditions. We weren't favoring Buddhism. There were symbols related to most major faith traditions in the session room. We were not focusing on a single religious tradition."

When Griffiths and I spoke, the teams at Hopkins and NYU were still analyzing the data from the roughly two dozen religious professionals who participated in the study, which includes follow-up research a year after they took the psilocybin. He declined to give any hints at their conclusions, or provide a breakdown of the religious affiliations of the subjects. They hoped to publish a paper on the study sometime in 2023. The year we spoke, Griffiths was diagnosed with cancer, undergoing treatments and facing his own mortality.

"I'm interested in secularized spirituality," Griffiths said.

"You can strip all the beliefs away and just get down to the basic fact that we find ourselves as these sentient creatures walking the Earth. We can touch and feel things. We can see things. We can speak and express complex ideas. And yet the only thing that we can ever really know is that we are aware that we are aware."

"That's the ground truth of it. And from that—for me—there arises this deep mystery as to what is going on there. What is this project of life about? We don't know the answer to that. No one does. Science doesn't answer that. It's the human condition. We are born into this mystery. Many of us get wrapped up in narratives about our lives that distract us from the mystery. But there is something about these experiences, from the way I see them, that speaks to that deepest mystery."[9]

CHAPTER 3
MYSTIC CHRISTIAN REVELATION

The Rev. John Mabry, a retired pastor with the United Church of Christ, has spent his life thinking and writing about the mystical core of the Christian tradition and how to help others navigate that territory. He has mixed opinions about the use of psychedelics as a spiritual path.[1]

"Mystical experiences interrupt life-as-usual and say, 'Hey! There is more to this than you thought.' Some people are going to go after that 'more.' That's what divine mystery is after—inviting people into that deeper interior reality. But these experiences aren't just an end in themselves—they're a glimpse into where we are going.

"Many people start on a mystical path because of their experiences on psychedelics. They can really be useful in that way. But if the person is just having the experience and not choosing to go deeper with it, it's a bit like having a one-night stand. The divine wants us to have a deeper relationship than that."

Like Rabbi Art Green, profiled in the previous chapter, Rev.

Mabry believes that mainstream religious institutions have failed to provide a viable path for the last few generations of spiritual seekers, whether or not they use psychedelics to connect with the divine. "We suck at talking about mysticism," he said in an interview. "We have this rich mystical tradition and we completely ignore it."

Mabry, who now lives in New York and teaches at the interfaith Chaplaincy Institute in Berkeley, said Catholics are better than Protestants in teaching about Christian mysticism—but both have a long way to go. He notes that the vast majority of both active and lapsed Christians are unaware of the rich mystical traditions in the Christian faith, such as Ignatian prayer, the early Gnostic Christian movements, non-canonical writings like the Gospel of Thomas, and such medieval mystics as Julian of Norwich, Meister Eckhart, and Mechtild of Magdeburg.

"Martin Luther was a deep mystic, but our Reformation heritage is all intellectual. There is no mysticism to it whatsoever," he said. "If you don't know about it, you can't pursue it. Christianity itself is a deeply mystical religion. Mysticism is at the heart of the religion. In becoming human, Jesus brought the Godhead into union with creation. That's a deeply mystical teaching. When a person is baptized, that person becomes one with Jesus. The body of Christ isn't a metaphor. It's a living reality."[2]

Mabry was born in a southern California suburb in 1962 and raised in the Southern Baptist Church. "I was so wounded by the fundamentalism in my upbringing," he said. "I was terrified of God." In college, Mabry turned to a more progressive and liturgical form of Christianity—the Episcopal Church. He felt called to the priesthood, but couldn't afford to attend an Episcopal seminary. After some years ministering in a small

Catholic-but-not-Roman movement, he was accepted into the United Church of Christ as a pastor.

His college years also found him experimenting with psychedelics. He dropped acid a few times, did some magic mushrooms, and became "an enthusiastic cannabis fan."

"In college, I was still pretty estranged from God and the church. I had some mind-blowing experiences, but I kind of compartmentalized them. I came to understand them better later on."

Along the way, he wrote a series of books about his journey, including *The Monster God: Coming to Terms with the Dark Side of Divinity* and *Growing into God—A Beginner's Guide to Christian Mysticism*.

In more recent times, Mabry has explored the psychoactive properties of ketamine. "My ketamine experience was very spiritually affirming. My understanding of God has changed. There is this mystery behind the universe, and our religious traditions are metaphors and symbols that point at that larger reality. Our religious traditions are like user interfaces on a computer. The guts of a computer are a completely mystery to me, but because I have this user interface, I can get a lot of work done. This is what religions do for us. We enter into relation with mystery and create meaning.

"When you do psychedelics, you get a glimpse of unmediated mystery that is really beyond comprehension. I don't see that as different from what my religion is pointing to, but it's on a scale where I can't do too much with it. The images and metaphors of my tradition help me to cozy up to this mystery, to make it approachable—it's more of a mediated relationship. Because of how we are structured psychologically, some of us need a face in order to be in relationship with that mystery. For me, the face of that mystery is Jesus."

Since the earliest days of the Jesus movement, followers of what would be later known as "Christianity" have been debating "Who was Jesus?" Or more to the point, "Who gets to decide?" Was he the Jewish messiah, a Palestinian revolutionary, a charismatic faith healer, or a gnostic mystic? Was he the founder of the Roman Catholic Church or one's personal Lord and Savior? Was he a wandering wisdom teacher, the only Son of the One True God, or the semi-mythological founder of a Greek cult formed around the ingestion of an entheogenic potion?

This debate dates all the way back to the early Jesus movement and the suppression of Gnostic communities in the first centuries of Christendom. Then, as now, mysticism and unauthorized prophecy were considered dangerous by the institutional church. The clearest example of this is the suppression of the Gospel of Thomas, a non-canonical text that has a pedigree at least as strong as the stories contained in Matthew, Mark, Luke, and John.

The Gospel of Thomas was among a treasure trove of ancient texts unearthed in 1945 not far from Nag Hammadi in Upper Egypt. The only complete copy we possess was written in Coptic, translated from a Greek original. Fragments of the Greek version were first discovered earlier in the twentieth century. There is no account of a virgin birth, miracle stories, or bodily resurrection in this version of the life of Jesus. It is simply a collection of 114 wisdom sayings attributed to the man.

As a thought experiment, try reading some of these sayings as a means of understanding the source of the healing behind psychedelic-assisted therapy and spirituality.

> "I am not your master. Because you have drunk, you have become intoxicated from the bubbling spring which I have measured out."

"Two will rest on a bed: one will die and the other will live."

"If you bring forth what is within you, what you bring forth will save you. If you do not bring forth what is within you, what you do not bring forth will destroy you."

"Let him who seeks continue seeking until he finds. When he finds, he will become troubled. When he becomes troubled, he will be astonished, and he will rule over the all."

"When you make the two one, and when you make the inside like the outside, and the above like the below, and when you make the male and the female one and the same… then you will enter the kingdom."

"Recognize what is in your sight, and that which is hidden from you will become plain to you. For there is nothing hidden which will not become manifest."

"Many are standing at the door, but it is the solitary who will enter the bridal chamber."

"Split a piece of wood, and I am there. Lift up the stone, and you will find me there."

"Why do you wash the outside of the cup? Do you not realize that he who made the inside is the same one who made the outside?"

"Become passers-by."

What is so striking about these passages is how modern they sound, how familiar to those of us who are more comfortable with the methods of psychotherapy than the religions of belief. Jesus is not telling us what to believe in the Gospel According to Thomas, but inviting us to find our own hidden truth.

There's a Zen-like quality to these sayings. Bible scholar Elaine Pagels tells a story of how she was having tea one October afternoon at the San Francisco Zen Center, about a year after the 1979 publication of her best-selling book, *The Gnostic Gospels*. Pagels was sitting with Richard Baker, who at the time was the leader of that pioneering Buddhist meditation center. He told her the story of how, as a young man, he'd left Boston and went to Japan, entered a Buddhist monastery, and became a disciple of Zen master Shunryu Suzuki Roshi, the founder of the SF Zen Center. "Had I known the Gospel of Thomas," Baker said, "I wouldn't have had to become a Buddhist!"

It's not surprising that Baker, a convert to Eastern mysticism, would resonate with the Gospel of Thomas. Another text from this Christian sect, written around 200 C.E., the Acts of Thomas, even claims that the apostle himself traveled to India and found many converts. Even today, many Christians in India see Thomas as the founder of their church. But this openness to the idea that we may find the divine in our own experience—that in a sense we *are* God, that there is no separation between us and the divine—was de-emphasized by later church leaders.

Here's how Mabry describes that mystic vision in his book *The Way of Thomas—Insights for Spiritual Living from the Gnostic Gospel of Thomas*: "Thomas' Jesus is trying to prod us into a state of unitive consciousness, in which we realize: the unity of God with all things (including we human beings), unity within the self, and our mystical unity with one another."

Mabry describes that realization as "at once slippery and simple," perhaps a bit like the revelations one might have on a properly prepared and responsibly facilitated trip on 5-MeO-DMT, ketamine, magic mushrooms, or LSD.

IN THE TUMULTUOUS SIXTEENTH CENTURY, a Dominican friar named Giordano Bruno argued that the universe was infinite and had no celestial body at its center. He believed in the transmigration of the soul, also known as reincarnation. His execution by the Roman Inquisition on February 17, 1600, which prefigured the more famous heresy trial of Galileo, made him—despite his clear spiritualist bent—one of the early martyrs of modern science.

Bruno, who entered the Dominican order in 1563 and was first branded as a heretic in 1576, travelled throughout Protestant England and continental Europe preaching the "new philosophy."

"Unless you make yourself equal to God, you cannot understand God," Bruno preached. "Make yourself grow to a greatness beyond measure...free yourself from the body; raise yourself above all time, become Eternity, then you will understand God," he wrote. It is within our power to strip "veils and coverings from the face of nature," to illuminate those who "could not see their own image in the innumerable mirrors of reality which surround them on every side."

Statements like this lead some to wonder whether Bruno's mix of revelation and grandiosity was fueled by the ingestion of a Holy Eucharist that contained sacred plant medicines with psychedelic properties. Brian Muraresku argues just this in his 2020 bestselling book *The Immortality Key—The Secret History of the Religion with No Name*. Muraresku subscribes to the "pagan continuity theory." That's the speculative idea that a secret tradition dating back to ancient Greece and the Eleusinian Mysteries has been kept alive by an underground network of witches and wise men through use of mind-expanding plants and drugs. What passes for Holy Communion in the Catholic church today, he suggests, is just a pale imitation of these secret age-old rites. Today's wafer and wine, Muraresku writes, can be seen as a "placebo Eucharist."

Muraresku argues that Bruno may have been enlightened by "drugs that the Vatican perceived as a heretical imitation of its own Eucharist, which it specifically convicted both Bruno and the witches of blaspheming." At least some of the countless men and women condemned by the Inquisition were employing "drugs that were considered so unquestionably superior to the traditional Christian Eucharist, however, that the wizard (Bruno) and his sisters were willing to trade their lives for the 'highest and final illumination' that could only be delivered by a homemade Eucharist."[3]

It's hard to find a theologically trained Christian scholar who will endorse the pagan continuity theory. Professor Thomas Cattoi, an authority on Christian mystical traditions at the Jesuit School of Theology in Berkeley, said there is no evidence that psychoactive plants had anything to do with Bruno's heresy trial. Even Mabry, a Christian mystic on the theological edge, calls Muraresku's theories about pagans, drugs and Christianity "a bunch of nonsense."

"I had the misfortune of reading *The Immortality Key*," Mabry told me. "I didn't appreciate the church-bashing. The church is an easy target, and for good reasons—the Inquisition, Crusades, pogroms. These are all horrendous things that should not be swept under the rug. But if you want to bash the church, write that book. If you want to speculate about entheogens, write that book."[4]

Muraresku's theories about a secret psychedelic tradition in Christianity—and the controversies they stir—are nothing new. In 1970, the British Bible scholar John M. Allegro published *The Sacred Mushroom and the Cross*. He argued that many of the stories and characters in the Bible—Jewish patriarchs, Jesus Christ and even the various names for God—are verbal puns tracing back to a secret Sumerian code language describing an ancient fertility cult centered around the worship of a sacred magic mushroom, the red-topped *Amanita muscaria*.

"Every aspect of the mushroom existence was fraught with sexual allusions, and in its phallic form the ancients saw a replica of the fertility god himself. It was the 'son of God,' its drug was a purer form of God's own spermatozoa than that discoverable in any other form of living matter. It was, in fact, God himself, manifested on earth. To the mystic it was the divinely given means of entering heaven; God had come down in the flesh to show the way to himself, by himself."[5]

Allegro speculated that the "historical Jesus" described in Matthew, Mark and Luke never existed. He was a creation of later church fathers trying to purge the cultic mysticism of the early Jesus movement, whose mythic origins are better seen in the fantastic visions and revelations in the fourth gospel account provided by followers of John.

These were not just the wild-eyed theories of some 1960s hippie high on drugs. In fact, it seems that Allegro himself had not even experimented with psychedelics. After serving in the Royal Navy during World War II, Allegro trained to become a Methodist minister, but instead wound up with a degree in oriental studies at the University of Manchester. He went on to teach a course in Old Testament and Inter-Testamental studies at that school. In 1953, he was named as the first British representative on an international team working on the translation and publication of the Dead Sea Scrolls. Those manuscripts, discovered in the mid-1940s in the Qumran caves on the northern shore of the Dead Sea, dated from the third century BCE to the first century CE. Written in Hebrew and Aramaic, they shed new light on the ancient Jewish sects like the Essenes, whose communal structure and theology appear to have deeply influenced the ministry of John the Baptist and early followers of the Jesus movement.

Allegro's agnosticism clashed with the orthodox ideas of the Catholic priests and other Christian scholars who worked with him to translate and understand the Dead Sea Scrolls. They gravitated to the orthodox assumption that Jesus was the unique and historical "son of God," while Allegro argued that the best way to understand the New Testament was to see it as a blend of myth, mysticism, folklore and history.

His 1956 book, *The Dead Sea Scrolls*, would sell more than 250,000 copies over the next four decades. By the time he died, of a heart attack on his 65th birthday in 1988, Allegro published thirteen books, including in 1979 *The Dead Sea Scrolls and the Christian Myth*. But it was the 1970 release of *The Sacred Mushroom and the Cross* that nearly destroyed his career. Fourteen British scholars denounced him. He resigned from his faculty position at the University of Manchester. His publisher apologized for releasing the work. The historian Philip Jenkins has called the book "possibly the single most ludicrous book on Jesus scholarship by a qualified academic."

Equally unimpressed was R. Gordon Wasson, a New York banker and self-trained mycologist who played a key role in the dawning of what we are now calling "the psychedelic renaissance." In 1957, *Life* magazine published a lengthy illustrated account of Wasson's "discovery" of a magic mushroom cult among the indigenous Mazatec people in the mountains of central Mexico. Over the next few decades, that story and later accounts would inspire thousands of beatniks, hippies and other spiritual seekers to embark on mushroom missions or peyote pilgrimages across Mexico—establishing a psychedelic tourism industry that continues today with ayahuasca adventurers seeking shamanic wisdom in remote South American outposts.

In an interview in 1985, about a year before he died, Wasson praised Allegro as a "brilliant man" who should be respected and esteemed for his role in translating the Dead Sea Scrolls. At the same time, Wasson accused Allegro of making numerous linguistic errors in *The Sacred Mushroom and the Cross*. He "jumped to unwarranted conclusions on scanty evidence," and then "made the unforgivable blunder of selling the manuscript to *The News of the World*," a British tabloid that serialized and sensationalized the work.[6] One could argue that Wasson did the same thing in his *Life* magazine account of the Mexican mushroom shaman Maria Sabina, who later came to regret her decision to ever let Wasson into her sacred circle.

By the time Allegro published his speculations about the psychedelic origins of Christianity, Wasson had moved on to studying the role that entheogens played in the development of religion in the Far East. In *Soma: The Divine Mushroom of Immortality*, published in 1969, Wasson posits the *Amanita muscaria* mushroom fueled the ritual drink referred to in the ancient Rig Veda scriptures of India. About a decade later, Wasson turned his attention to the psychedelic rites in ancient Greece. In 1978 he teamed up with Albert Hofmann, the Swiss chemist who first synthesized LSD, and Carl Ruck, an authority on Greek myth and ethnobotany, to publish *The Road to Eleusis: Unveiling the Sacred of the Mysteries*. Their book—largely ignored at the time of its publication—sought to identify the ingredients in the psychoactive potion that fueled secretive rites conducted for nearly two millennia at Eleusis, a pilgrimage site outside Athens.

Few movements in the long history of esoteric religion rival the Eleusinian Mysteries for their influence and staying power. They began around 1500 B.C.E. as a local cult around Demeter, the Olympian goddess of the grain harvest, but spread throughout the Greco-Roman world until these rites were largely suppressed in the fourth century with the rise of Christianity as the official religion of the Roman empire. In his contribution to *The Road to Eleusis*, Hofmann argues that the potion used in the mystery rites could have easily contained hallucinogenic ergot, a fungus growing on wheat and barley—the very grains that Demeter blessed as the goddess of the harvest. In his Swiss laboratory, Hofmann analyzed the ergot from wheat and barley and found that they contained traces lysergic acid amide, a less potent relative to LSD.

This obscure collaboration by Albert Hofmann, Gordon Wasson and Carl Ruck is the work that Brian Muraresku resurrected and popularized in *The Immortality Key*. He argues that the barley-based potions at Eleusis, the *kukeon;* the *soma* of ancient India; and the Dionysian wine of Roman rites were all spiked with psychoactive plants and fungi. He cites depictions in Christian art, along with intriguing, yet somewhat sketchy archeological evidence, to argue that esoteric sects within Christianity continued this entheogenic communion for centuries.

The three main chapters of *The Road to Eleusis* were based on papers that Hofmann, Wasson and Ruck presented at the Second International Conference on Hallucinogenic Mushrooms, held on the Olympic Peninsula in Washington state in the fall of 1977. In his presentation, Gordon Wasson recounts how his fascination with mushrooms began fifty years before, in the summer of 1927. He and his new bride, Valentina "Tina" Pavlovna, were on their honeymoon in the Catskill mountains in New York. At the time, Wasson was working as a newspaper man in the financial department of the *Herald Tribune*. His wife—who had fled Russia with her family in 1918, when she was just seventeen—had gone to medical school in London and was just establishing her pediatric practice in New York. During a walk in the woods, Tina collected a wondrous array of wild mushrooms, edible but not entheogenic, lovingly identifying each of them by their Russian names. Gordon, like many Americans, suffered from mycophobia. Tina, who reveled in her native mycophilia, cooked some up for an evening meal. Gordon not only declined to taste her culinary creation; he worried that he might wake up in the morning as a young widower. Tina survived, bemused by her new husband's paranoia, and went on to inspire the couple on a decades-long study of how various cultures fear, appreciate or worship what Gordon had once dismissed as poisonous "toadstools."

The couple's vocation led Wasson and Allan Richardson, his friend and photographer, to Mexico in the summer of 1955 to document the work of Maria Sabina, the Mazatec Indian who shared her psychedelic "Little Saints" with these two freelance journalists. Twenty years later, here's how Wasson remembered the all-night ritual in Sabina's village in the mountains of Oaxaca. "All you see during this night has a pristine quality: the landscape, the edifices, the carvings, the animals—they look as though they had come straight from the Maker's workshop. This newness of everything—it is as though the world had just dawned—overwhelms you and melts you with its beauty. Not unnaturally, what is happening to you seems to you freighted with significance."[7]

In his 1977 paper, Wasson seemed open to the idea that the "lowly" fungi has long inspired poetry, philosophy and religion, all the way back to ancient Greece. "Some are shocked that the key even to religion might be reduced to a mere drug," he writes. "Out of a mere drug comes the ineffable, comes ecstasy. It is not the only instance in the history of humankind where the lowly has given birth to the divine."

Yet ten years later, shortly before his death, Wasson was extremely reluctant to discuss the role that psychedelic mushrooms or other entheogenic plants may have played in the early Christian church, or that they may play today. In an interview in 1986, Robert Forte asked Wasson what he thought of the idea that psychedelics could "revitalize religion by renewing a sense of the sacred in our society." He replied, "I do not like to deal with such immense subjects. I have my own thoughts, but they are not really worth repeating. I do not like to discuss them."[8]

This reluctance may be explained by later revelations that the Vatican was one of Wasson's clients during the 1940s and 1950s, when he worked as international banker for J.P. Morgan. According to one of Wasson's banking colleagues, "Gordon used to have private audiences with the Pope."[9]

In their book *The Psychedelic Gospels—The Secret History of Hallucinogens in Christianity*, Jerry and Julie Brown argue that "the unmasking of the Wasson-Vatican connection calls into question everything Wasson ever wrote to justify his position on the absence of entheogens in the Judeo-Christian tradition." This includes Wasson's attacks on John Allegro when *The Sacred Mushroom and the Cross* was released in 1970. Noting that Wasson was long considered "the leading authority on the study of entheogens and religion," the Browns write, "It is as if it were suddenly revealed that the foremost climate change denier of our day—a scientist whose research was highly respected and widely reported—had for decades been on the payroll of ExxonMobil."[10]

In a letter to the *Times Literary Supplement*, Wasson dismissed Allegro's credentials, saying he was "not a mycologist, but, if anything, a cultural historian."[11] Wasson also got into a public debate with Allegro about the sole illustration in the first edition of *The Sacred Mushroom and the Cross*. That would be a photograph of a twelfth century fresco on the wall of a ruined chapel in Plaincourault, France, built by the Knights of the Order of Malta upon their return from the Crusades. It depicts Adam and Eve covering themselves in the Garden of Eden, flanking a giant "mushroom tree." A snake winds its way up the trunk of a tree. "There the *Amanita muscaria* is gloriously portrayed, entwined with a serpent, whilst Eve stands by holding her belly," Allegro writes. "The cunning reptile prevails upon Eve and her husband to eat of the tree, whose fruit 'made them as Gods, knowing good and evil.' (Gen. 3:4)"

Wasson cites an art historian to bolster his argument that "the plant in this fresco has absolutely nothing to do with mushrooms."[12]

In the end, John Allegro and Gordon Wasson were both imperfect pioneers in the still evolving search for a psychedelic tradition within the Christian faith. In my view, Allegro was onto *something*, but his desire to categorically dismiss Christianity as an esoteric fertility cult widely missed the mark. Wasson is also suspect, and not just because of his Vatican connections. Some fringe historians of the early psychedelic movement argue that Wasson was working with the CIA as part of a vast "mind control" conspiracy to placate the populace away from political action.[13]

In his 1986 interview with Forte, Wasson himself conceded that the CIA approached him back in the 1950s, but that he declined to cooperate. "The CIA thought that they might be able to apply this to war, and they wished to investigate it." Wasson acknowledges that CIA put a chemist "on my trail" from the Geschickter Foundation, one of several front groups set up by U.S. intelligence agencies to secretly fund psychedelic research in the 1950s.

In *The Immortality Key,* Muraresku continues to present only *speculative* evidence that Jesus *could* have been passing around psychedelic wine at the Last Supper.

In an online conversation with the author, the director of Harvard's Center for the Study of World Religions pointed out that while there may have been Greek mystery cults or Dionysian movements communing with magic mushrooms or ergot-spiked beverages, Muraresku's book does not really link this to early Christian practices. "I'm not here trying to protect Christianity from the evidence of psychedelic use," director Charles Stang said. "I expect we will find it, but I don't think we have found it, and that's an important distinction to make." Muraresku concedes the point. "All I present is wonderfully attractive and maybe even sexy circumstantial evidence for the potential use of a psychedelic sacrament amongst the earliest Christians."[14]

Stang then questioned Muraresku's belief that psychedelics are so significant that they might usher in a new Reformation.

"How can you reasonably expect the church to recognize a psychedelic Eucharist?" Stang asked. "Do you think that by calling the Eucharist a 'placebo' that you're likely to persuade them?"

Muraresku, who writes that he has not personally experimented with psychedelics and "still considers myself a good Catholic boy," stressed that he was not trying to antagonize the church. But it's worth pointing out, he added, that according to one poll, 69 percent of American Catholics do not believe in the doctrine of transubstantiation—that the bread and wine of communion literally becomes the body and blood of Christ.

"I see a thirst, especially in young people, for real experience," Muraresku replied. "What comes to my mind is how, if at all, can psychedelics enhance faith or reinvent Christianity. I don't think that psychedelics are coming to replace the Sunday Eucharist...If there is a place for psychedelics, I would think it would be in one of the sacred containers within monastic life, or pilgrims who visit one of these monastic centers. Or maybe in palliative care...I can see psychedelics as being some kind of extra sacramental ministry that potentially could ease people at the end of life."

It's easy to get lost amid all the theological, political and historic debate over what role, if any, sacred plant medicines have played in Christianity over the last two millennia. From the earliest decades of the Jesus movement, there have always been many "Christianities" operating simultaneously and often in conflict with one another.

Once you start looking for mushrooms in Christian art, you start to see them everywhere. The intriguing presence of fungi in the frescoes can be easily blown out of context and misrepresented, just like Jesus himself. At the same time, the evidence in Christian art can't be explained away. Just open to the insert of color photos in *The Psychedelic Gospels.* Exhibit A: a basket of *Amanita muscaria* mushrooms in the Basilica of Aquileia in Italy, circa 330. Exhibit B: An angel holding a mushroom in the fresco of a tenth century church in what is now Turkey. Exhibit C: Jesus blessing a bowl of mushrooms in the Great Canterbury Psalter in England, circa 1200. Exhibit D: numerous mushrooms tucked into the stained-glass windows in Chartres Cathedral in France, circa 1210.

There's evidence, and then there's belief. In the end, it really comes down to belief. Entheogens may have played *some* role in the inspiration of mysticism in the early church and within the long Roman Catholic tradition, just like they do among today's devotees in the Santo Daime church and the Mazatec mushroom cult in Mexico. These movements have always operated, almost by definition, on the mystical edge of the Church Triumphant. Sacred plant medicines have the power to inspire seekers to take control of their own spiritual lives, which has, and continues to threaten the guardians of orthodoxy and the powers that be.

"Religion finds this bitter pill impossible to swallow," writes Clark Heinrich, the author of *Magic Mushrooms in Religion and Alchemy*. "Governments declare it illegal and fill prisons with the 'illegally religious' just as surely and irrationally as the Romans filled their jails with early Christians... The informed use of entheogenic, consciousness-enhancing plants and drugs presents a direct and powerful challenge to any system that seeks to spoon-feed the masses with false ideals of nationalism, racism, sexism, or predigested religion, and this is precisely the reason entheogens have been criminalized."[15]

Like Gordon Wasson and John Allegro, Heinrich tends to see *Amanita muscaria* mushrooms hidden everywhere in the sacred texts of the great religions of India and the Middle East. His search for the Holy Grail was inspired by a mind-blowing experiment back in 1977, when he and a friend learned how to safely prepare and consume the "fly agaric" every day for thirty-one straight days, going to extraordinary efforts to intensify the psychedelic experience.

This California ethnobotanist presents an intriguing, albeit speculative, reimagining of how the earliest followers of Jesus may have found inspiration and communion in magic mushroom elixirs or ergot-infused bread. I was especially taken by Heinrich's sharp critique of the moribund state of the current church. "The mystery of Jesus is that there is no longer a Mystery in Christianity; everything has been explained," he writes. "The official position of all the differing branches and sects is the same, one of the few things they agree on: Christianity today has no secret rites. Yet Jesus himself was the head of a heretical mystery cult, the initiates of which met secretly to share sacred food and drink while their master explained to them the hidden meanings of his teachings."[16]

No one has a monopoly on spiritual truth. Perhaps the

work over the last half a century of the Browns, Heinrich, Allegro, Wasson, Hofmann, Ruck, and Muraresku can inspire another look at what we think we know about the carpenter from Nazareth. Jerry and Julie Brown end their adventure story across the churches of Europe with a scene when they return to the U.S. to visit Jerry's mother at a nursing home in Tuscon. Just a few days before her death, Marion Brown has a dream that "God is a river of love that flows through the universe. All I have to do is let go into that river."

"This too is the message of Jesus Christ, a message of love and compassion that reverberates through the centuries, uplifting the spirits of billions of people," they write. "Undeniably, one of the most expansive effects of entheogens is their ability to open our hearts to the wellspring of boundless love that flows within each and every one of us."[17]

SPECULATION about an alleged tradition of psychedelic Christian Communion often ignores the *actual* history of mysticism in this ancient faith. "I resent the reduction of mysticism to psychedelic experience," Mabry told me. "There is so much more to it than that. It completely dismisses the mystical power that the Eucharist has had for a couple thousand years. It's a willful dismissal of centuries of powerful mysticism in the Christian tradition."

Mabry makes a good point, but it's also true that some aspects of Christian mysticism may be employed as roadmaps to prepare for a psychedelic journey and to integrate the insights one might have.

Cattoi, the expert on Christian mysticism at the Jesuit school in Berkeley, suggests that one such roadmap could be the *Philokalia*, a collection of long-forgotten writings that were put together by two monastics in the late eighteenth century. The texts themselves were written in the fourth to fifteenth centuries. They present a way of looking at consciousness that differentiates between deductive and intuitive modes of experiencing the world.

"We have an underlying faculty that is noetic—a direct perception that doesn't go through inference and reasoning," Cattoi told me. "It's a form of intuitive knowledge. It's a faculty that allows you to perceive the presence of the divine in the world without the mediation of reason."[18]

These Christian mystics lay out three stages of preparation to develop mystical insight. They are purgation, learning not be controlled by your passions, followed by illumination, or "seeing the world the way it really is," both of which lead to a unitive consciousness and the direct experience of the divine.

"It is a kind of de-centering of the self where you get to the point where you can be fully present in the world by the cultivation of attention," Cottai said.

Cottai, who is married and has a family, was on sabbatical in Bologna when we spoke over Zoom. This Italian-born scholar has lived in the U.S. for twenty years after studying in England. He moved to the Bay Area after earning his PhD at Boston College. He has served as the co-chair of the Mysticism Group for the American Academy of Religion and was one of the founding members of a Buddhist-Christian dialogue group sponsored by the Catholic Theological Society of America.

He sees psychedelics as "a way to re-access our own noetic capacities," but only if it is "grounded within a broader framework of ethical reconfiguration of one's own inner life and is part of a whole program of growth."

Cattoi is familiar with the emerging psychedelic movement, having also trained to become a licensed therapist at the California Institute for Integral Studies in San Francisco, which has long been a mecca for those interested in studying the spiritual or therapeutic potential of psychoactive drugs.

"In the *Philokalia*," he said, "you find breathing exercises or other psycho-physical exercises, such as fasting, to bring about altered states" of consciousness, but no references to sacred plant medicines or fungi. So he sees little evidence to support the pagan continuity theory or the idea that there is a secret tradition of Christian psychedelic communion.

"You are never going to find a scholar of early Christianity who will agree with that," he said. "You can't base this on finding some frescoes in France. Sure, maybe some painters in France may have taken psychedelics and smuggled some images of mushrooms into their work. But you can't say that's the grounds for a tradition that is clearly not there."

Hunt Priest, the Episcopal clergyman who found Ligare, the psychedelic Christian society described in chapter one, thinks the church should be open to re-examining its history, including the possibility that magic mushrooms or other sacred plant medicine may have once been an ingredient in Holy Communion. He called Muraresku's book "an important work that's worth considering."

"Christianity has been influenced by every culture it has encountered, especially Greek culture and Greek mystery religions," Priest told me. "I think we should have a very expansive conversation in Christianity about exactly what Brian's bringing up and not be afraid of it. We shouldn't be afraid of new knowledge. If psychedelics were somehow part of our history, that would inform my own Christian experience."[19]

CHAPTER 4
PSYCHEDELIC CHAPLAINS

My friend Tony Hoeber is a psychedelic chaplain. He's sitting across the table at Saul's, a Jewish deli not far from the University of California at Berkeley campus. We're not here because his father and my mother were Jewish. We're here this afternoon because I realized that I can't write a chapter about psychedelic chaplains without putting Tony in the story. We've had lunch at Saul's many times before, and we've had this conversation more than once, but this time we're not just here for the crispy latkes, creamy hummus or the killer corned beef on rye. This time the voice memo app on my phone is running and Tony is talking "on the record."

Medicine chaplaincy is Tony's second career, following a decades-long run as a tech pioneer in Silicon Valley. We're both pushing seventy. Tony didn't have time to wait for the theological establishment, the medical community, or the U.S. Food and Drug Administration to wake up to the fact that psychedelics drugs and sacred plant medicines can be a wonderful—and sometimes terrifying—way to explore the mysterious contours of the human soul.

We were both born in 1953, but neither of us set foot in a synagogue when we were growing up. My mom had a tough New Jersey childhood in the 1920s. She did *not* want to even talk about her Jewish ancestry. Tony's dad would discuss the Jewish religion, but only with derision. "My father was a cantankerous atheist," Tony said between bites of his omelette. "He was German Jewish. They wanted to escape the ghetto and escape being defined by religion. Their project was to worship at the altar of science. Religion was for stupid people. Religion was laughable." His dad was trained as an economist, but spent most of his professional life working as a nuclear war strategist for think tanks like the Rand Corporation. Herman Kahn, the physicist who provided the inspiration for the Peter Seller's character in the black comedy *Dr. Strangelove*, was an occasional dinner guest at their family home in Palo Alto.

"I've had to do a lot of work over my life healing from trauma and a family seriously affected by mental illness. My family business was nuclear war strategy. My stepmother was the Undersecretary of the Army under Reagan and built up the U.S. stockpile of offensive chemical weapons. Think about it, Don! That's the family business!" [1]

Tony stayed away from psychedelics and other drugs as a teenager and for most of his life—except for one acid trip during his undergraduate years at the University of California in Santa Cruz. "It was a bit too much for me," he recalled. At the same time, Tony was a spiritual seeker. He joined an ancient Sufi order when he was twenty-one and studied that mystical path for more than four decades. "I was spiritual in this 'New Age' way, but I wasn't a dabbler." He went on to have a successful career as a user interface designer in Silicon Valley, where he also started a foundation to support the work of the Dalai Lama.

He stumbled into the psychedelic subculture during a trip to Brazil in 2012, when he was studying somatic trauma therapy with a teacher who invited him to an ayahuasca church affiliated with the União do Vegetal, or UDV. That's one of two major psychedelic church networks with branches in South America and the United States. (We'll explore the other one, Santo Daime, in the next chapter.) During his first ayahuasca journey, Tony had a powerful vision of his biological mother, who committed suicide when he was ten years old. "This full-on angel was holding my mother for two hours and whispering to me, *She's all right. She's okay…and also, by the way, Tony, you're okay, too. Your life has not been ruined. It's fine.* It touched me deeply. It was like those were the words I'd needed to hear my whole life."

Returning to the U.S., he realized there was a UDV church not far from his home. He joined, and spent seven years as a member. "They're very structured. They have communion with ayahuasca at eight o'clock on the dot every other Saturday. They end at exactly twelve midnight. They have an order and a way of doing everything. It's kind of like Catholicism meets the Pentagon meets ayahuasca. They wear uniforms. They're like the military. It's all hierarchical. You advance by conforming."

In the end, Tony was asked to leave. He'd started exploring other ways of working with entheogens, and eventually enrolled in an underground psychedelic therapy training program. Tony also graduated in a separate, above-ground certificate program and was ordained as a chaplain by the interfaith Chaplaincy Institute in Berkeley.

There you have it—medicine chaplain.

"One of the things I learned at the institute is that I have what is known as an 'eclectic faith style.' I've studied

Buddhism and Sufism very deeply, and a lot of other things, like Jungian analysis. I've put them together. In religion, eclecticism has a bad reputation because it's seen as superficial. I get that. But if you do it seriously over many years, then you integrate all these things in your own way, I see it as a creative process."

Tony's underground training was a three-year program in which he was one of eighteen students in his class. They would meet one day a month for the entire day to "get the download" from their teachers. Students would get experience facilitating psychedelic sessions with MDMA and magic mushrooms by pairing up and sitting for one another. "At the end, the way they described it, this was an ordination. So I have a dual ordination, one underground with them and one above-ground with the Chaplaincy Institute. My atheist father would be rolling over in his grave."

My friend estimates that he's led sessions with about 180 clients over the last five years. Most of them have been fifty years of age or older. They're struggling with different kinds of trauma, substance abuse, sex and love addiction. "I've had a number of older clients who are at the 'empty nest' stage of life. They've worked for maybe twenty or thirty years, are nearing the end of their career and are now wondering what's next. They want to find a new passion, a new purpose to engage them. It's an existential problem. As a chaplain, I'll have conversations about making meaning. It may be a spiritual thing, or not. Some of them could care less about religion. But they need to find meaning in their lives."

TONY WAS the first person I met who referred to himself as a "medicine chaplain." But there's now a robust conversation underway about bringing trained chaplains into the burgeoning network of those offering psychedelic-assisted therapy and spiritual care.

Chaplains are often ordained in a specific religious tradition, but are also trained to care for people of other faiths—or no faith—in hospitals, prisons, universities, and the military. Whether it's counseling families who have just lost a loved one in the emergency room, or dealing with soldiers recovering from the horrors of war, chaplains help people get through the most traumatic events of their lives.

"Chaplains already have significant training in being present to transpersonal experience," said the Rev. Jamie Beachy, a longtime chaplain and ordained minister in the United Church of Christ, a liberal Protestant denomination. "People at the end of life often have deep experiences of those who have passed on before, or communication with God in their dreams. That territory is very familiar to chaplains."[2]

After working for years as a hospital chaplain and training for inter-religious spiritual care, Beachy now directs the Center for Contemplative Chaplaincy at Naropa University in Boulder, Colorado. She is also working as a co-therapist with the Multidisciplinary Association for Psychedelic Studies (MAPS) as part of its ongoing clinical trials of MDMA-assisted therapy to treat survivors of extreme trauma.

In Berkeley, chaplaincy is one approach offered in a training program organized by the University of California's Berkeley Center for the Science of Psychedelics. In 2022, the Berkeley center launched a Certificate Program in Psychedelic Facilitation. It is designed for "advanced religious, spiritual care, and healthcare professionals working in areas such as chaplaincy, ministry, medicine, nursing, mental health counseling, psychiatry, and social work."

Rachael Petersen, the psychedelic strategist whom we met

in chapter one, has been trying to build bridges between psychedelic guides and seasoned chaplains. "A lot of these research institutions and universities that are doing psychedelic work have trained chaplains—but they are not talking to one another. I have spoken to so many professional spiritual caregivers who sit with the dying and the dead, or who sit with people going through profound, non-ordinary experiences. We want to integrate that with psychedelic research."

The Rev. John Mabry, profiled in the previous chapter, trains chaplains at the interfaith Chaplaincy Institute in Berkeley, where psychedelics have also become a new topic of conversation. "There is definitely a spiritual component to psychedelic work," he said. "You're having an unmediated experience of the All. It's going to have religious connotations. Training people to companion others through that experience seems an awful lot like chaplaincy to me."

Mabry believes psychedelics have a role to play in spiritual awakening, but not in regular church practices like Sunday worship. He does see a place for these tools in chaplaincy and spiritual direction, which often resembles psychotherapy. "That's an individual thing. Churches are about communal experience."

"Psychedelics can help anybody (not just Christians) come to an awareness that there is more to the universe than scientific rationalism. But is that going to revitalize the Christian church? I don't think so. Nevertheless, there are individuals Christians who might be awakened to the mystical reality inherent in the universe. It would be a good thing if they follow it up and move into a more mystical expression of their faith."[3]

Mabry himself has not worked with psychedelics as a chaplain or spiritual director. Rabbi Michael Ziegler, on the other hand, has spent the last four decades leading ceremonies in expanded states of consciousness. He's also ministered to people on their death bed, and says the same skills are needed when sitting with someone having a psychedelic experience.

When working with people who are dying, "you listen to people and offer your presence. You meet them where they are. You're not going for some bedside conversion." In working as a psychedelic guide, "the natural impulse is to get involved or try to be helpful or make meaning. Really skilled sitters have a super light touch. It's a meditative experience to sit in service for someone for eight hours on a mushroom trip with a booster. You'd think it's super easy, but trust me, it's not."

Ziegler is a disciple of the late Ralph Metzner, who worked with the psychedelic pioneers Leary and Alpert at Harvard in the early 1960s. Metzner and others stressed that psychedelics are non-specific amplifiers of whatever preconceived ideas and expectations a person brings into a session. "On psychedelics, you are extraordinary suggestible," Ziegler said. "Anything you drop in there is going to blossom."

"Today, it seems like everyone and their dog are calling themselves entheogenic guides and psychedelic therapists," he said. "Training programs are popping up everywhere, and most offer no practice experience in leading trips—just clinical theory. We had the meditation fad. We have the yoga fad. Now we have the psychedelic fad. People are out there saying, 'the mushrooms told me to be a shaman. Are you kidding me? It's all so immature. And it's dangerous."[4]

Ziegler hopes new programs like those at University of California, Naropa, and being considered at Harvard, Emory University and the Graduate Theological Union in Berkeley, will bring a bit of gravitas to this work. "This is not the Church of the Frisbee. It's Harvard. It's Berkeley. This is the beginning of a serious conversation about how to sacralize the use of psychedelics in service of meaning making. In ten years, these initiatives will bear fruit."

A few years ago, Ziegler was called to the death bed of a longtime rabbinical friend. The night before the rabbi died, he sat with his family through a MDMA experience in which they reaffirmed their love, forgiveness and reconciliation for their father.

"He passed away the next day, and went out with a low-dose shot of ketamine, in place of morphine," Ziegler said "For me, that's the holy of holies."

THEOLOGICALLY AND POLITICALLY PROGRESSIVE SEMINARIES, such as the Unitarian Universalist's Starr King School for the Ministry in Oakland, have led the way in conversations about chaplaincy and psychedelics. Adjunct faculty member Ayize Jama-Everett, who teaches a course called "The Sacred and the Substance," hosted a webinar where graduates of the school talked about their spiritual callings.

The Rev. Emily Webb, an ordained Unitarian Universalist minister and hospice chaplain, said she hoped that those pushing the medical model of psychedelic care could be more open to ancient wisdom traditions and "indigenous ways of knowing."

"We have an enormous crisis in mental health—particularly among young people, the elderly, and populations that are marginalized," she said. "Therapy that costs $225 an hour, once a week, is really failing…I hope I can be an advocate for moving the medical model more toward a community-centered, peer-led model, a decriminalization model, a shared-knowledge model."

Anthony Graffagnino, an Interfaith-Quaker chaplain, has

worked with researchers at UCSF Medical Center, working to develop "a spiritual assessment model for chaplains serving in psilocybin therapy contexts."

The panelists were asked how their psychedelic experiences have come to shape their theology. Graffagnino's answer:

"I now believe that that god, the goddess, the divine, the sacred that we encounter comes from within and without. The magic and the beauty that we encounter comes from within and without. The healing and insight and wisdom that we encounter comes from within and without."

Chaplaincy and psychedelics was also one of the topics discussed at a "Religion and Psychedelics Forum" sponsored in 2022 by the Chacruna Institute for Psychedelic Plant Medicine. Religion scholar Erik Davis, who convened the conference with Chacruna leader Bia Labate, said the model of the "chaplain" is in some ways a better one than that of the "therapist."

"One of the great problems with psychedelic mainstreaming is, 'Who are going to guide all these people? All these training programs are popping up and naive people are jumping into the space without the decades-long practices that are helpful for doing this. The model of chaplaincy is a beautiful and powerful one to approach how people are able to integrate psychedelics into their lives...The secular mantra of wellness, of psychological healing, is great, but it only goes so far. We have no choice but to dive into these sacred waters."

In a panel at the Chacruna conference, Petersen and Beachy were joined by two other chaplaincy experts. The Rev. Caroline Peacock, an Episcopal priest, is the director of Spiritual Health at Winship Cancer Institute of Emory University in Atlanta. She is doing research on the experience of chaplain guides in psychedelic assisted therapy in healthcare settings.

Kamal Abu-Shamsieh, a professional chaplain who is a

Muslim, is also an assistant professor of practical theology, and director of the Interreligious Chaplaincy Program at the Graduate Theological Union. Abu-Shamsieh, who said he has no personal experience with psychedelics, stressed that the efforts to train psychedelic chaplains through his GTU program and University of California at Berkeley and San Francisco are still in the early stages.

"Not all faith communities support the use of psychedelics, including my community," he later explained. "Members of these communities might seek psychedelic experiences, and there is a need to train chaplains to offer religiously and ethnically competent care."

Leaders at the center in Berkeley, and at the medical school at University of California in San Francisco, say their new training program will allow some trainees to safely and legally be administered psilocybin through a study approved by the U.S. Food and Drug Administration.

It will "offer opportunities for healthy volunteers to access first-hand experiences" with psychedelic drugs. "Medically eligible trainees may volunteer as participants in the study, thereby increasing their personal knowledge of psychedelic substances and their capacity to support others accessing psychedelic care."

Dr. Brian Anderson, a faculty member at UCSF and an investigator affiliated with the Berkeley center, stressed that "participation in the certificate program is neither a requisite for, nor a guarantee of, being selected for volunteering as a subject in psychedelics research." Because of legal restrictions, some early training programs in this field, such as one at the California Institute for Integral Studies in San Francisco, have not been able to openly offer these first-hand experiences.

UC education professor Tina Trujillo, who heads the Cal training program, said the new effort will have "a nuanced understanding of psychedelic facilitation," along with "skills-based training in mental health, professional spiritual care, and the scientific research that seeks to understand how psychedelics may affect health, well-being, and the mind."

Organizers of the Berkeley center have sought to incorporate the scientific, spiritual and shamanic—approaches that, as we've seen in previous chapters, have increasingly found themselves at odds in the "psychedelic renaissance." According to the course prospectus, graduates of the program "may also be eligible to participate in an immersive learning experience in Oaxaca, Mexico."

"This pilgrimage will provide first-hand educational experiences with the historical and spiritual origins of the Mazatec mushroom traditions, from the perspectives of local indigenous healers, scholars, and other community members."

The Berkeley center reports that it has received $7 million from five philanthropic donors, including a five-year, $5 million pledge from Blake Mycoskie, a philanthropist and founder of Tom's Shoes, to advance the center's mission of research, training, and public education about psychedelics and their roles in society." Author and fitness expert Tim Ferriss has donated $800,000 to pay for psychedelic reporting fellowships at the UC Berkeley Graduate School of Journalism. Another donation of nearly $1 million came from the Steven & Alexandra Cohen Foundation. That money will be used to develop an online "Psychedelics 101" course by UC Berkeley neurologist David Presti, and other faculty affiliated with the center.

Those familiar with the internal debates around the new psychedelic studies program at Cal told me that a proposed partnership with the nearby Graduate Theological Union has been particularly fraught.

"The GTU board was very reluctant to engage in this sort of

enterprise—for all sorts of reasons," said Thomas Cattoi, the professor at the Jesuit school, which is part of that seminary consortium. "Churches and seminaries are very wary (of psychedelics) because they think it's a shortcut. You are trying to get to the end without doing the work. There may also be fear of competition."[5]

There are also tensions around the "wokeness" one finds in both the psychedelic and academic world—especially in the San Francisco Bay Area.

"We went to a workshop that some of the people at UC Berkeley sponsored. We felt they weren't interested in our input very much," the seminary professor told me. "They just wanted to do their own thing and then pretend to consult with us. They wanted me to come and teach Christian spirituality for three hours, and do that from an indigenous perspective. I said, 'You can't teach Christianity spirituality in three hours and do it from an indigenous perceive because there is so much more that I have to talk about.'"

"Why *just* from an indigenous perspective?" I asked.

"That's the whole problem," Cattoi replied. "I said I'd want to teach about the early Christian period, and they said, 'Oh, no. We can't support 'whiteness.' So I pulled out. You can't ask me to teach Christian spirituality and then say you can't do that because it's 'whiteness.' It's unfortunate. Everything is so ideological. If we read early Christian authors, it's 'whiteness.' But we can read other authors, like Buddhist authors, because that's not 'white' and that's fine… This kind of racial essentialization is so self-destructive. I find it very difficult. I'm white. I'm a man. I'm from Europe. So they can immediately cast me out in the name of Euro-centrism."

Cattoi's break from the Berkeley bubble and his sabbatical in Europe reminded him that "the church is much larger than what might be going on in the Bay Area."

Nevertheless, just the fact that the University of California even has something called the Berkeley Center for the Science of Psychedelics is fairly amazing, but in some ways not surprising. In 1965, just a couple years after the fellows at Harvard College dismissed the infamous Timothy Leary as a lecturer in clinical psychology, he issued a prophesy.

Leary, who began his doctoral studies at UC Berkeley in 1947, is remembered today for a controversial psychedelic career that began with a poolside magic mushroom trip in the fall of 1960 in Cuernavaca, Mexico, with *Psilocybe cubensis* scored off an old *curandera*, a Mexican shaman Leary called "Crazy Juana." Speaking at a 1965 conference in San Francisco, Leary said, "I predict that within one generation we will have, across the bay in Berkeley, a Department of Psychedelic Studies. There will be a dean of LSD."

It was a long time coming, but it is here and it is now.

IN 2022, medicine chaplain Tony Hoeber felt the call to travel to a remote region of Oaxaca, Mexico to work with native healers who use psilocybin mushrooms in a tradition that blends folk Catholicism and indigenous spirituality. He and a group of pilgrims made their way to a Mazatec village, Huaulta de Jimenez. This is the same outpost Gordon Wasson visited in the 1950s for his famous *Life* magazine encounter with Maria Sabina.

We're well into our lunch at Saul's. Tony's been talking a mile a minute and has barely touched his omelette. I've finished my latkes, grilled eggplant and am just scooping up the last bit of hummus with a remnant of pita bread. My last questions to my friend are about Tony's recent pilgrimage to

Mexico, which he looks back on as a mixture of the sacred and profane.

"For me, it was like, okay, I'm gonna go to the source and I'm going to see for myself, right? You go to Mexico City, then you go to the city of Oaxaca, and then you take a bus way up into the mountains, in this little town that's clinging to the hillside with steep winding streets. And it's raining, I mean *really* raining. Images of Maria Sabina are all over the town. It's sort of become an identity for the town."

"They say, 'Here, take your mushrooms, be courageous, do your work.' And then they pray and they pray in Spanish and Mazatec. They pray to Jesus and to Mary, and they sing to Jesus and Mary. This is an actual communion. It's not considered to be symbolic. It's not an idea. It's not a game. It's real."

Tony's description of his experience reminded me of an interview I had some years ago with another pilgrim who has made multiple visits to this Mazatec village. "At first, it was very challenging to me because of my strict Catholic upbringing," she told me. "When they'd pray to Mary and Joseph and Jesus on the cross, I was resistant. But then the symbols became archetypal. Jesus was the mushroom, the messenger of the divine. Catholics believe that in communion, you eat the flesh and blood of Jesus. The Mazatec eat the flesh of the earth and God in the body of the mushroom. It's a sacred communion."[6]

Despite his secular Jewish upbringing, or perhaps because of the universalism of his mystical Sufi lineage, Tony did not struggle with the Christian imagery in the Mazatec mushroom ceremony.

"I had this experience of Jesus dedicating his life, his passion, for others. I had a felt experience of that. Has that changed my life? I don't know. But it's very precious to me. It's enlarged my understanding of life. It's beautiful. Is it enlightenment with a capital E? No. Did it make me a better person? I don't know. It hasn't made me worse. I went down and I did have a profound experience, and I'll have it with me for my whole life."

At the same time, Tony saw another side of the psychedelic tourism business in Oaxaca, the disagreements and competition between indigenous families and among family members in the village. "It's a large family of five sisters doing this work. One of their brothers tried to chase us away. 'Get outta here! You're not welcome!' Part of it is this dysfunctional family fighting with each other. There is the economic competition for the North Americans with money coming down here."

I asked Tony if he felt like he had to travel to this poor Mexican village to get permission to sell his mushroom therapy to affluent clients in Marin County. Was he worried that he was somehow engaged in "cultural appropriation?"

"I did have some of that," he replied. "I was trying to work that out. What is legitimacy? In any healing capacity, you have to have a sense of empowerment. Where does that come from? You know, the doctor has his white coat and his medical degree. So what's my authority? Do I pretend that I have feathers or descend from some indigenous lineage? No. But there's nothing inferior about me. Indigenous people are not above me, or somehow purer or closer to the source. There's me and my life and my heart and my mind and my experience and my motivation. That's what's real—a sincere motivation to help people."

CHAPTER 5

AYAHUASCA CHURCHES EMERGE

It had been more than two decades since federal agents in Oregon seized their psychedelic sacrament and arrested the spiritual leader of the Church of the Holy Light of the Queen. "They had no clue as to what they were getting into," recalled Jonathan Goldman. "They didn't know what ayahuasca was. They thought they were coming into a drug den and were going to find people shooting up."[1]

Oregon has come a long way since that raid in the spring of 1999. Now all eyes are on the Pacific Northwest as that state became the first in the nation to regulate the production and completely legalize the use of psilocybin—albeit in a limited way.

For nearly two years, the Oregon Psilocybin Advisory Board has been working out the details on how to implement Measure 109. That ballot initiative, passed in November 2020 with fifty-six percent of the vote, made supervised psilocybin mushroom trips legal, starting on January 1, 2023. A separate ballot measure passed in that same election, Measure 110, has already made the possession of small amounts of all previously illicit drugs—including heroin and cocaine—punishable by what amounts to a parking ticket with a $100 fine. And even that fine is waived if the arrested person agrees to a health screening from a recovery hotline.

Together, the saga of the Ashland-based Church of the Holy Light of the Queen, and the deliberations of the Oregon Psilocybin Advisory Board, illustrate two ways that psychedelics are gaining mainstream acceptance.

One route is through the ballot box and the city-by-city, state-by-state reform of repressive drug laws. The other is a religious freedom battle waged through the courts, which is how Church of the Holy Light of the Queen became one of the first spiritual communities in the nation (other than the peyote-based Native American Church) to legally and openly engage in entheogenic communion.

Goldman's small congregation—a northern outpost of Santo Daime, a South American religious movement—first made headlines in May 1999. That was when U.S. Customs agents seized a shipment of ayahuasca tea sent from Brazil, where the church is based. "They took me to jail. They invaded my house," Goldman said in an interview. "They took my children out of class and threatened to take my kids away. But they didn't pursue my prosecution."

Santo Daime is a new religious movement founded in the Amazon in the 1930s by Raimundo Irineu Serra, who was born in Brazil to parents of African descent, and died in 1971. The grandson of slaves, he is known by his followers as Master Irineu. His church grew out of a series of ayahuasca-inspired visions the founding prophet had during eight days of jungle solitude.

Church teachings—a mix of folk Catholicism, African animism, spiritualism, and South American shamanism—are transmitted through hymns sung during ayahuasca ceremonies. Irineu was raised in the Roman Catholic Church, so perhaps it's not surprising that one of his earliest visions was of the Virgin Mary, whom he called "the Queen of the Forest." Here's how the church's website sums up its theology today: "We praise God, Jesus Christ, saints, angels and spiritual beings of many cultures, especially Christian, Indigenous and African ones."

Goldman grew up in a Jewish family in Detroit. Like other Jewish psychonauts, he has struggled to reconcile his religious heritage with the Christian, syncretic, or perennial philosophy trappings in much of today's psychedelic movement. He recalls in an essay about how his first Santo Daime experience in a remote Brazilian valley forced him to confront "Jewish PTSD."

"I found myself in a strong altered state in the presence of this big cross in the middle of an altar table. I started to have thoughts about the pogroms my Russian ancestors had gone through, and it was like, 'Holy shit! Here I am in this totally bizarre place and they're going to kill me.'" Then he looked a bit closer and saw that the cross was sitting on the base of a six-pointed star. He told himself, 'the star I can deal with. I'm going to ignore the cross so I don't run out of here screaming.'"

It has taken years of prayer and meditation, much of it in the "true light" of the ayahuasca experience, but he has learned to "resolve this conflict inside me between the cross and the star because I don't want to live in fear. I resolved the ancient war between siblings inside of me."

Looking back, Goldman now sees his first Daime experience as a difficult but necessary way to confront "all of one's fears, opinions, and misconceptions about oneself and reality —transforming them into spiritual knowledge."

Goldman's Church of the Holy Light of the Queen is one of hundreds of ayahuasca churches and spiritual groups that have established themselves in North America over the last thirty years. Some are aligned with different branches of the Santo Daime movement. Others are organized under the stricter governance of another Brazilian sect, the União do Vegetal, "Union of the Plants" or UDV. Still others are independent or loosely aligned with a purported Latin American lineage.

In 1999, the same year that federal agents arrested Goldman, thirty gallons of ayahuasca tea was seized in a raid at the UDV church offices in Santa Fe, New Mexico. Both churches filed lawsuits against the government action and eventually won the right to operate legally under the provisions of the Religious Freedom Restoration Act, a federal law that grew out of government harassment of the Native American Church, which uses peyote in its spiritual ceremonies.

Those court victories have led to the theory that anyone has the right to legally use ayahuasca or other sacred plant medicine in religious rituals in the United States. In Goldman's opinion, they do not—unless they prove in court that they are a legitimate religion in the eyes of the government. Meanwhile, federal agents have continued to seize shipments of the tea and arrest self-proclaimed ayahuasca shamans who openly advertise their psychedelic services.

"It is not legal to use ayahuasca in the United States," Goldman said. "It is legal for us to use Daime (ayahuasca) because we and the UDV could prove, for real, that we are an extension, a branch, of a religion. There are three things you have to have if you go to court. You have to be taking care of people. You have to be taking care of the sacrament. And you have to have a spiritual lineage."

In 2007, Goldman and the members of his church split off from the main Santo Daime network in the U.S. in a schism Goldman now describes as "difficult but friendly." The following year, his Ashland church successfully sued the federal government, arguing that their use of psychoactive tea was protected by their religious rights under the Constitution.

Goldman said his Ashland church has about 45 regular dues-paying members. Before the COVID pandemic, its ceremonies would attract between forty and sixty people, and perhaps double that if a Santo Daime leader was visiting the church from Brazil.

Like many seasoned veterans, Goldman has mixed feelings about the explosion of entheogenic exploration in today's psychedelic renaissance. On the one hand, he believes that "it's not the government's business to regulate what people do with their bodies." On the other hand, "there are people who go to Peru for three weeks, come back with ayahuasca [and start leading ceremonies] with no idea what they are doing."

"This is a delicate thing we are doing—dropping the veils of consciousness," he said. "The veils are there for a reason, and dropping them is a serious, serious, serious thing to do. I've handed thousands of cups of Daime to people. When I hand them that cup, it's the most sacred, serious and blessed thing I can ever do."

BEFORE STARTING HER OWN CHURCH, Vicki Kraft sat in several different psychedelic circles, including some affiliated with the Santo Daime. Some of these ceremonial leaders, she recalls, were doing great work. But there were sharp disputes over whether to seek legal status or establish a formal network of ayahuasca churches in the U.S. There were also allegations of sexual misbehavior.

"One group I was with were followers of a man who was a perpetrator," Kraft said. "I couldn't be part of that…I prefer to be part of a group with a strong structure, that does this work openly, with the lights on, and is more communally based."[2]

Today, Kraft is the spiritual leader of the Flower of the Divine Mother, an ayahuasca church in Southern California that is a branch of Goldman's Oregon church. That gives Kraft's congregation clear legal protection. In 2014, five years after the Oregon church won its case, Kraft's Southern California congregation formally applied to the Drug Enforcement Administration to legally operate under the provisions of that same federal law.

"We went to the DEA website and filled out an application," she said. "Within six months, it was approved. They asked me a lot of funky questions. A local DEA agent came to my house and said, 'Okay, where are you going to store this [ayahuasca]? I said, 'I'm going to put it in this refrigerator, and they said, 'Okay. Get a lock for it.'"

Kraft then applied for an importer's license so she and other members of her church could travel to Brazil and return with ayahuasca tea. It only took two weeks. "They were very cooperative. I've had several audits by DEA agents who come in with an adversarial tone. I have to remind them that we are not a pharmacy. They don't really know what we're doing because they're not used to auditing churches. They are used to auditing pharmacies."

As Marc Gunther reports for Lucid News, other emerging psychedelic churches have not had such an easy time dealing with the DEA. In Arizona, two ayahuasca churches—the Arizona Yage Assembly and the Church of the Eagle and the Condor—sued the U.S. government, arguing that DEA rules amount to unconstitutional prior restraint upon their right to practice their religion. Both churches had shipments of ayahuasca seized and destroyed by U.S. customs and homeland security agents. "You don't have to ask the government if you can practice your religion," argues George Lake, a lawyer who had written about entheogenic churches and their constitutional rights. But other legal experts urge caution. "This area is rife with legal risks," said Allison Hoots, a lawyer who works with the Chacruna Institute. "Almost every church that I work with is underground."[3]

Soul Quest, an ayahuasca retreat center in Florida, charges $999 to participate in a weekend ceremony, with another $200 for "add ons." In 2021, the DEA denied its request for an exception to legally operate under the provisions of Religious Freedom Restoration Act. Nevertheless, Soul Quest continued to openly advertise and operate as the Ayahuasca Church of the Mother Earth.[4] In rejecting Soul Quest's application for an exemption to federal drug laws, the DEA cited the fact that the organization appeared to be operating more like a money-making retreat center than a church with regular members holding sincere religious beliefs.

"Soul Quest does not require individuals to profess belief in Soul Quest's Ayahuasaca Manifesto…before participating in a Soul Quest ayahuasca retreat," the government said. "Nor does Soul Quest require or expect individuals to have any continuing involvement with Soul Quest or membership in any congregation or other group of believers, and, in fact, individuals frequently participate in only one of Soul Quest's ayahuasca retreats." Thus, the DEA concluded in its ruling, "membership in Soul Quest appears to be a purely pro forma matter to obtain access to ayahuasca, rather than an expression of sincere religious devotion."

The drug agency contrasted Soul Quest's operation to the Church of the Holy Light of the Queen, citing the Oregon federal district court's ruling in favor of Jonathan Goldman's congregation. That church "attempts to select only those who are serious about the Santo Daime religion, and to turn away would-be recreational users or thrill-seekers." It also noted that the Oregon church, as opposed to the Florida retreat center, "demands a serious commitment of time and energy from members, requiring attendance three or four times per month at services lasting several hours and sometimes almost all night."

According to Bia Labate, the executive director of the Chacruna Institute for Psychedelic Plant Medicines, there are now hundreds of "sincere and legitimate plant medicine communities" in the United States. While many believe they have the freedom to practice their religion under the protection of the First Amendment to the Constitution, neither the Religious Freedom Restoration Act (RFRA) nor the DEA provides clear guidelines as to what constitutes a "religion."

"We are interested in 'freedom' in the broadest sense, meaning the freedom to experience the full range of our potential, and the liberty to engage in psychedelic culture and to explore its possibilities within the social realm," she said.

Labate, a Brazilian anthropologist living in the San Francisco Bay Area, made that statement to mark the release of Chacruna's 84-page *Guide to RFRA and Best Practice for Psychedelic Plant Medicine Churches*.[5] The document analyzes the key religious freedom rulings issued by the federal courts in the hope that underground churches can present a strong legal case should law enforcement agents ever raid their church, seize their sacrament or arrest their shaman.

For ten years, Vicki Kraft's church has met twice a month in a big downstairs room in her home in Redondo Beach.

Kraft was born in the San Fernando Valley in 1952 and grew up in a Jewish family. Like many in her Baby Boomer generation, Vicki got interested in meditation as a teenager. She went to college in San Jose, where she started experimenting with psychedelics and having deep mystical experiences.

"Of my college crowd," she told me, "I'm the only one who stuck with psychedelics. I am a religious person. I believe in God. Not that many people talk about God. I wouldn't say I was identified with the Jewish religion per se. Santo Daime is very Christian-based, and to this day, I still struggle with that. It's not about Jesus Christ. It's about Christ consciousness… What attracted me most was that I could have my own experience with the divine. That, to me, was what I was seeking—to see the other side of the veil."

Like many mainstream churches, the Flower of the Divine Mother struggled to keep the flock together during the COVID pandemic. "In the beginning, we had people saying, 'COVID's not real. I won't wear a mask. We lost some people who were anti-vaxxers. It's sad. Before COVID we had 40-45 people. We were turning people away. Our last work [ayahuasca ceremony] was fifteen people. Not everyone is ready to come back."

It's unclear what the future will bring for Kraft's congregation and the larger ayahuasca movement. She's saddened and a bit bemused by all the infighting among the larger Santo Daime groups in the United States.

"They drink gallons and gallons and gallons of Daime [ayahuasca] and they still haven't figured out how to love their brothers and sisters. It's in every hymn we sing. 'We should be one. We should be together. I'm a bit of an outcast. The Daime structure in Brazil is more hierarchical. I don't resonate with that. My group is the Flower of the Divine Mother. It's all about the divine feminine."

Labate, who has studied the Santo Daime movement, noted that this emerging religion is just one of many institutions that have faced allegations of sexual misconduct by spiritual leaders and cover-ups by church authorities—in both psychedelic communities and mainstream institutions like the Roman Catholic Church and the Southern Baptist Convention.

"Unfortunately, the systemic cover up of sexual abuse is not only a Brazilian trend or something practiced by patriarchal Christian religions in the Global South. It is also found in progressive religious and academic circles in the United States, right in the core of the so-called psychedelic renaissance," said Labate.

Officially, Kraft is the madrinha of her flock and Jonathan Goldman of Ashland the padrinho of his larger network. Kraft downplays her spiritual status. "I'm not a shaman. I just lead the works." She's never tried to make a living off ayahuasca. She's always had a day job, working as a licensed marriage and family therapist. "We're non-profit. Nobody is making money off this. We all have jobs and our own source of income. We just need to make ends meet. People donate what they can."

In recent years, Kraft has watched the commodification of psychedelics turn into something of an elitist pastime—with people charging hundreds or thousands of dollars to participate in a ceremony. "That's exploiting the medicine," she said, "and exploiting the movement."

How can explorers of ayahuasca and other entheogens step back from the sometimes bizarre experiences generated by psychedelic drugs and sacred plant medicines? Is this revelation or delusion? How are we to know if we are connecting with divine truth or just fueling our own spiritual grandiosity?

One particularly fascinating and informed account of this struggle comes to us from G. William Barnard, a professor of religious studies at Southern Methodist University in Dallas. He is the author of *Exploring Unseen Worlds: William James and the Philosophy of Mysticism* (1997) and *Living Consciousness: The Metaphysical Vision of Henri Bergson* (2011). In his book, *Liquid

Light: Ayahuasca Spirituality and the Santo Daime Tradition (2022), the professor comes out of the closet as a fifteen-year devotee of that church, seeking to balance his academic skepticism and religious faith.

Like many baby boomers, Bill Barnard had his psychedelic baptism as a teenager, courtesy of a couple of mind-bending LSD trips. Unlike most of us, he has spent a lifetime trying to understand these and later experiences as both a scholar and a believer.

What are we to think when we find ourselves "so utterly immersed in the extremely rich, poignant, breathtakingly beautiful flow of what's happening, both inside and outside?" Try as we might, Barnard suggests that "there's simply no place for some detached, sit-back-and-watch witness to calmly remember it all."

Barnard took a deep dive into the devotional, visionary world of ayahuasca, Brazilian-style. He struggles, for example, to understand the meaning, message and reality of a shimmering green lizard-being, majestic and noble, adorned with magnificent swoops of gold and red around the eyebrows, or a "Green Goblin" figure that flies around cackling, leering and laughing.

Barnard views his revelatory visions through the lens of the renowned American psychologist Williams James (1842-1910) and the French philosopher Henri Bergson (1859-1941). As explained in his landmark book *The Varieties of Religious Experience*, James argues that visions produced by drugs or other spiritual practices are not necessarily just delusions or hallucinations conjured up by the brain. Perhaps the brain is somehow tuning into pre-existing states of awareness, a "continuum of cosmic consciousness." Bergson also argues that "consciousness is not a function of the brain," that it can and does transcend physical boundaries.

To Barnard, the strange entities and wondrous beauty he encounters on ayahuasca are not simply delusions or projections created by his own mind. "In fact, we can argue that they might well be manifestations of a more profound, more inclusive quality of perception."

Barnard is associated with a branch of the Santo Daime movement that embraces spirit mediums to communicate with "suffering spirits." These are seen as the ghosts of human beings who are stuck on this plane of existence. They still have business to do here on Earth, such as unfulfilled desires, a longing for revenge or issues with addiction. "Due to the lack of a physical body," he writes, "they are not able to fulfill that endless craving."

This particular Santo Daime sect is strongly influenced by the Umbanda movement, one of several Afro-Brazilian spiritist movements embraced by millions of devotees of South American mix-and-match religion. During a reporting trip to Brazil back in 1987, I spent one wild night in communion with Umbanda priest, Jose Alberto Nunes, and fifty members of his flock gathered in a large room behind his house in Fortaleza, Brazil. No psychedelics were involved in these rites, which seemed to be fueled instead by the consumption of copious amounts of alcohol.

Here's the top of my report published in pages of the *San Francisco Examiner*:

"Conga drums, Catholic prayers and African chants fill the temple with a hypnotic Afro-Brazilian beat. Clouds of incense barely conceal a pervasive aroma of spilled rum and human sweat. Suddenly, Expedita Pinheiro feels herself going into a trance. Her 14-year-old daughter keeps her from tumbling onto the floor as Pinheiro spins into the center of the room like a whirling dervish. There, Pinheiro is surrounded by other mediums possessed by the spirits of gypsy whores, Indian chiefs, and old black slaves. Young women smoke five cigarettes at a time. Gay men possessed by the spirits of female prostitutes prance among the worshippers. Mediums overtaken by the spirits of old drunks guzzle bottles of beer. And Jesus Christ looks down on it all from a Technicolor crucifix atop an altar overflowing with dime-store icons."

It's hard to imagine mixing a powerful psychedelic beverage with these rites, but that's exactly what this Dallas-based religious studies professor has been doing for the past fifteen years. Barnard assesses his ayahuasca experiences through William James three-fold test for discerning the validity and value of a spiritual revelation. Does it have "immediate luminosity,' "philosophical reasonableness,' and "moral helpfulness?"

For him, life as a Santo Daime devotee—at least potentially—passes all three tests. Barnard also believes that Santo Daime would pass muster with Huston Smith, the respected scholar of comparative religion and one-time associate of Timothy Leary. Smith stressed that "religion is more than a string of experiences." He wondered whether a true psychedelic church would emerge out of all the entheogenic experimentation of the baby boomers of the 1960s and 1970s—"something like the Eleusinian Mysteries" of ancient Greece. Barnard argues that Santo Daime is exactly such a "modern-day mystery school."

After venturing deep in the Amazonian jungle, and consuming large amounts of ayahuasca at marathon and often arduous Santo Daime ceremonies in Brazil and in the U.S., Barnard has moved from the camp of "agnostic skepticism" to the view that "reality seems to be much stranger and more mysterious than I once thought."

"The world suddenly opens up; magic, mystery and wonder return—the iron cage of modernity no longer feels quite so inevitable," he writes. "We begin to see with great clarity how we had previously, unknowingly, been living in a Flatland, two-dimensional world, a world created by our limited assumptions and experiences."

In an interview over Zoom, I asked Barnard—who was raised in the Methodist church—what he thought declining mainline churches like the one of his childhood could learn from the burgeoning psychedelic renaissance.

"The major obstacle is for mainstream churches to let go of this sense that these substances are drugs and are inherently causing psychopathic hallucinations in people. Yes, the brain is being altered, but let's think of it as the brain switching channels on a TV. These substances have been used for thousands of years in an integral way in people's lives. Perhaps we can look at these less as pernicious drugs and more as sacraments. These substances can be a vehicle for God's grace in people's lives, to share God's presence and light and love in beautiful disciplined thoughtful settings."

And what can the psychedelic community learn from mainline religion?

"With the Daime, we already know the importance of discipline and commitment and having ongoing community," Barnard replied. "The 'spiritual but not religious' people want freedom. They don't want people telling them what to believe and what to do. But if you are making it up all yourself, the ego is running the show. But if you're spiritual, you don't want your ego running the show. There are all kinds of lessons you can only learn with a stable, institutional structure and a community. For the longest time, I didn't want anything to do with religion. I was spiritual but not religious. But I've come around. I think you need it for spiritual growth. When I came into the Daime, I'd say things like 'why do we have to sing all night?' Well, it's like being in a baseball game and saying I want five strikes, not three. You have to play within the structure."⁶

My first ayahuasca journey did not play out within the formal structure of this church, but it was in Brazil and did include the singing of songs from the Santo Daime.

Two dozen Europeans and North Americans—me included—came together in early 2014 at a retreat center a couple hours outside Rio. By the time we took the sacrament, we'd been living together for almost two weeks—exploring meditation, tantra, ecstatic dance, and various psychodynamic exercises designed to cultivate a deeper sense of *being*, rather than our normal state of *doing*. Some of us already knew each other from a previous "Art of Being" workshop in Greece, so we entered the psychedelic space with preexisting conditions of love, empathy, and connection.

Our ayahuasca facilitator was a fairly renowned Brazilian guitarist who took songs and other elements from Santo Daime ceremonies—stripping away some of their more overt religious or spiritist trappings. By the time I downed my first glass, I'd already read a lot about ayahuasca and interviewed a few ayahuasca devotees, so I was familiar with the popular idea that this tea is a "teacher" that somehow knows what we need to experience. Of course, I had trouble believing this. How can two plants brewed into a bitter tea have any kind of intention or directive knowledge?

Compared to many accounts that I've read or heard about, my visions during my two all-night ceremonies in the Brazilian jungle were relatively tame. At one point, a couple I had befriended over the previous two weeks morphed into living corpses when I looked at them across our circle of psychonauts. They were obviously struggling. I knew beforehand that they were dealing with recent deaths in their family and tension in their relationship. At one point, one of them was having trouble getting up and making her way to a bathroom that was a short walk from the expansive thatched-roof temple where we had gathering for the night. I got up and helped her find her way, taking her by her skeleton hand. Later, she told me that the being who helped her go to the bathroom was a fuzzy, friendly version of Donald Duck, webbed feet and all.

My main feeling during that first night was one of disappointment. I was not feeling or experiencing what I'd read about in other accounts—like heroic journeys across ancient landscapes of crystalline bliss. I caught myself resenting the fact that the facilitator had seemingly given me a relatively small serving of tea. I wanted to get higher, which is not an unusual state of mind when I begin to alter my consciousness. I saw no mythic beasts, giant insects or the Blessed Virgin Mary pointing me toward new ways of living. At one point, with eyes closed, I managed to see some sparkles of light, kind of like a string of white Christmas tree lights. The brightest light, which seemed to be saying "follow me," led me on a tour of my own brain. It was more of a feeling than a vision, but the experience was a bit reminiscent of the 1966 sci-fi thriller, "Fantastic Voyage," in which a small submarine and its crew are shrunk to microscopic size and injected into the blood stream of a brain-injured CIA agent. I'd seen the film when I was thirteen, which stuck with me in no small part because it featured my teenage heartthrob, Raquel Welch.

Raquel did not make a cameo appearance during this journey into my brain, but there was a sense that some other divinely feminine character—this time in the form of that bright light—was running the show and showing me the way. Let's call her "Mother Ayahuasca." At one point, she instructed me to stop at a place in my brain, or someplace above my brain, which was divided into two parts. My Addict Brain was having a conversation with my Higher Brain. I was just there listening. *Why do you always want more? Don't you see that your craving takes you away from experiencing life, not further into it? What you need is not more, but amour. More love, not more drugs.* This was not a new idea to me, but the way in which the message was delivered was qualitatively different.

It seemed like I had just scratched the surface of what I might learn from the tea, so when I returned home I connected with a Northern California-based friend of a friend who led ayahuasca journeys. Tom Pinkson is a shamanic teacher, psychologist and ceremonial leader. In the 1980s, he began a decades-long apprenticeship with a Huichol peyote shaman in central Mexico. He combines that knowledge with teachings he picked up from ayahuasceros in Brazil and other indigenous medicine elders around the world, plus a long career in counseling and hospice work. He also had a close relationship with Terence McKenna, the ethnobotanist and raconteur who helped popularize ayahuasca in the 1990s.

I would join Tom and his California tribe for three all-night ayahuasca ceremonies over the next year. The experience that has the most relevance to this book unfolded on my first journey. Fifteen of us had gathered in a home in Marin County. We began by revealing our intentions for coming here. One man was having trouble in his marriage. An older gentleman was struggling to make the transition to the next, and perhaps final, stage of life. A woman talked about the challenges she faced in her desire to, like Tom, be a "bringer of the medicine." I mentioned that I had recently stopped taking traditional anti-depressants and talked about my hopes that this medicine would give me new insight into my melancholy, helping me open my heart and feel joy.

When the time came to down the sacred brew, we individually approached an altar in the center of the circle and took part in a "Sweet Medicine Bowl" ritual Tom had learned from his Huichol mentor. Five empty bowls arranged in a line represented our grandparents, our parents, ourselves, our children and our grandchildren. To the side was a larger sixth bowl with grains and little pieces of chocolate. We each took a pinch from that bowl and placed some in the five bowls, which represent our ancestors and our descendants. Later in the ritual, Tom mixed all this grain and chocolate into a sweet soup, which was shared from a common bowl passed around the circle.

Looking back, I can see how this ritual inspired a subtle, slippery vision. At a certain point during the night, I suddenly felt like I was inside the mind of my grandfather, my father's father. He's the only grandparent I really knew as a child. Grandpa, a retired stock broker, bowling alley operator, and sports promoter, once known in the New York newspapers as "Big Al Lattin from Manhattan," lived with us during the final decade of his life. But this was my grandfather as a young man, in New York City, circa 1915, walking down Broadway a couple years before my father was born. There was no story. It was more of a feeling that the sadness I experience was an echo of his sadness. As soon as I tried to rationally understand this, to turn it into a story, to psychologize it, the feeling passed.

During my reporting for this book, I checked back in with Tom. It had been more than seven years since our ayahuasca ceremonies. Unlike the last time I wrote about Tom—when he was extremely private and guarded about the work he was doing—he was now comfortable with his real name being used in a public forum. He's been doing this work for over half a century, including with a spiritual community stretching back four decades.

Today, psychedelics are going mainstream, which this veteran explorer sees as a mixed blessing.

"Now everybody and their cousin is a psychedelic therapist, primarily using the therapeutic/medical model. It's disconcerting to me because it doesn't honor the spirit of the plants nor does it emphasize the importance of giving back to your community, to the Earth, and to the spirit world, which from a shamanic perspective is an important aspect of journey work. You get something to bring back to your tribe, to benefit people, to benefit life. That's the whole purpose. It's not for individual aggrandizement. I was taught by indigenous elders who held a community perspective. Their emphasis was on integrating what was learned into daily life interaction with each other. In my spiritual community we seek to live from and grow the love. We speak truth in a kind way, with authenticity, integrity, civility and generosity. We celebrate the good times with each other and support each other in the hard times, which is what sane communities do. The majority of people I work with today are seeking healing through connection and communion to a higher presence. Call it spirit, the universe, God, the Tao. We're forging a new understanding, a new relationship with spirituality from what they grew up with."

Personally, I did not feel called to join the Santo Daime Church nor Tom's community. But my ayahuasca-fueled vision of my grandfather walking down the boulevard a century ago did inspire me to spend the better part of a year trying to understand the life of my grandfather, and his father, and our forefathers. And I did the same for my maternal Jewish ancestors. I realized how little I knew about the childhood of the man I knew as a child, about his struggles as an orphan who found his way into New York City at the turn of the twentieth century. Going back further, I dug into the story of how our sixteenth-century Flemish ancestors fled the northern arm of Spanish Inquisition. I realized how long my family had been running from the oppressions of organized religion, only to become new oppressors as settler colonists arriving on these shores in the wake of the Mayflower.[7]

"We often have clogged pipes in our relations with our ancestors," Tom said in our most recent conversation. "It impacts the quality of our lives now, no matter what our background is. At one point your people get their asses kicked by others, and then go on to kick other people's asses."[8]

Sounds about right, Tom, but maybe it's time to stop running from the religion of my ancestors, to stop looking for spiritual sustenance in all the wrong places. Maybe it's time to try to understand my Jewish and Christian heritage in a new way. But first, I needed to make one more extended visit to the Church of Psychedelic Revelation.

CHAPTER 6

SACRED GARDEN CHURCH

Sacred Garden Church, an intriguing experiment on the eastern edge of San Francisco Bay, emerged from a network of drug-reform advocates who in 2019 persuaded the Oakland City Council to direct its police department to stop arresting people for using plant-based psychedelics like magic mushrooms and ayahuasca.

Sacred Garden calls itself "a multi-sacrament church." Included are magic mushrooms, plants containing such psychedelic compounds as mescaline and DMT, and also psychoactive chemicals like MDMA and LSD.

You can believe almost anything you want and join the Sacred Garden. Members of this "post-modern church" adhere to a "faith of least dogma." But they are required to at least be open to the possibility that psychedelics—used with care and respect—may provide access to the "divine."

This exploration is gently led by the church's senior pastor, Bob "Otis" Stanley, a Tennessee born-and-bred authority on the psychoactive properties of a dizzying array of plants and fungi. Stanley has ancestors with deep Quaker roots, but grew up in the 1970s in a conservative Methodist family. "I'm not a Christian. I'm not a Buddhist. I'm not an indigenous practitioner," Stanley said. "There is something that is divine, but we are not trying to define that."[1]

"Religions assert all kinds of things," said Stanley, who holds a master's of divinity degree from the University of Chicago. "Christianity will say after you die you go to heaven. Buddhism might say if you meditate like this for many lifetimes, eventually you'll have some nirvana. That's lovely. I don't know what happens when I die, but this I know. It is possible to have a direct experience of the divine—whether you call it satori, or God coming and saying 'hello.' We can have that experience in this lifetime…That's why we need these sacraments."

Some scholars and sociologists of religion see churches like Sacred Garden and the broader psychedelic renaissance as part of a transition from an era of word-based religion to a time of experience-based spirituality. In this view, psychedelics are a powerful force for revival—like the printing press was for the 16th century church reforms of Martin Luther.

Among those academics is Thomas B. Roberts, a professor emeritus at Northern Illinois University, who began teaching college courses on psychedelics in the early 1980s. Roberts, most recently the author of the 2019 book *MindApps*, said churches like Sacred Garden "can provide experiential depth to what had previously been abstract words."

"Ideas such as awe, sacredness, eternity, grace, agape, transcendence, dark night of the soul, born again, heaven and hell, divinity, blessedness, gratitude, adoration, faith and forgiveness may take on new depths of meaning," he said. "They become alive."

Over the last two years, Sacred Garden Church has grown to about 90 "confirmed practitioners," members who have gone through a three-month period of preparation that is required before they can participate in psychedelic ceremonies. That includes me, who briefly joined as part of my own entheogenic exploration and to offer an inside account of the congregation as a participant/observer.

The church is one of about a dozen congregations in the Sacred Plant Alliance, which seeks through self-regulation to promote ethics, accountability, safety and legal aid in emerging psychedelic communities. Most of its member organizations are still operating underground, or just starting to come out in the open.

Unlike the two ayahuasca-based churches profiled in the previous chapter, Sacred Garden has not sought an exemption to federal drug laws under the Religious Freedom Restoration Act. Nevertheless, Stanley and church attorneys assert that they "are practicing within the intent of religious freedom protections" offered by the First Amendment of the U.S. Constitution.

"As we are engaged in sincere religious practice, the burden is on the government to avoid interfering with our practice. To date, formally petitioning the government has required churches to stop their sacred practices while the petition is considered," he said. "Churches have waited for years with no response."

Stanley's psychedelic journey began in the 1980s with a series of teenage acid trips with some friends in the Smoky Mountains of Tennessee. "All the trees started going into patterns and moving toward me. The air became solid light. Everything became light and I was part of that—golden white light. These are things you can't explain, but eternity was present...So I recognize LSD as a sacrament by direct revelation."

Bob begins to tear up when he starts looking back on his

psychedelic baptism. "It's hard to talk about the most precious experiences of my life...when LSD opened that experience to me...to eternity, to the love of God. It helped me let go of suffering and become more loving. That was, without question, the experience of sacrament."

We are sitting in Bob's kitchen. He's one of several tenants living in an old red brick industrial building in the Oakland flats, not far from downtown. Before we sat down, he gave me a tour of his own sacred garden: dozens of plants growing in a variety of large ceramic and black plastic pots on what was once a parking lot and loading area for delivery trucks. Most of these plants contain some kind of psychoactive compound. "These are sacred plants of the Big Sky, the mescaline containing plants," he says, pointing to a stand of large vertical cacti. "People in the U.S. call them San Pedro, but that's a postcolonial name. Some now prefer to call them wachuma. They have Big Sky Spirit."

Later on my tour, I ask Bob which plants he uses to produce changa, a smoking blend at the center of the church's psychedelic initiation ritual. "Those are the deep forest plants," he says, reaching out to touch the leaves of a *psychotria alba* plant growing out of a black plastic pot. "The White Queen. Some people call it chacruna."

When I take a picture of the plant, Bob bursts into a song of gratitude, as he often does when giving his plant sermons. "Thank you. Thank you. Thank you," he sings. "Beautiful plants!"

Moving on, he stops to pay his respects to an ayahuasca vine, the other ingredient in his changa blend. "This one is three or four years old and survived a cold snap. I've got one inside that's fifteen years old. These tend to grow in shaded and wet areas. They help us to go deep within, to deal with things that need to be transformed. Deep forest plants help you go down and bring up things in your life and convert them to fruits and flowers or healthy things."

Bob's black cat, Bill, slinks around the potted jungle and starts nibbling on some long grasses which also contain DMT.

Later, sitting in his kitchen, Bob explains why he feels it's important to have a variety of psychedelic sacraments—some from nature and some from the laboratory. "We had a good friend who just did not respond to ayahuasca. He could drink five cups and nothing would happen. LSD was effective for him. Others don't respond to mushrooms, but do with wachuma. In our church, anything that helps us make a divine connection is required. Some people may have so much shame, and they just go deep into endless shame with mushrooms and hate themselves more. But MDMA might help them move through that and work with it...We're letting the city know what we are doing here with these practices, and that we consider all these things to be sacraments."

Bob Stanley was born in 1966 in Oak Ridge, Tennessee, home of the national laboratory run by the U.S. Department of Energy and originally built to develop the atomic bomb. His father, a doctor and chief of staff at the local hospital, raised his kids in the Methodist church, but was open to exploring various elements of the so-called "New Age" movement in the 1970s and 1980s. There were books by Carlos Castaneda (*The Teachings of Don Juan*) and Charles Tart (*Altered States of Consciousness*) in the family library, which Bob started reading at a young age. Bob first turned on during the "Just Say No" era of the Reagan administration. His father supported Reagan politically, but was also open to psychedelic revelation. In the 1990s, Bob and his dad both went to seminars at the Esalen Institute at Big Sur, and even traveled together to ayahuasca and mushroom retreats in Brazil and Mexico. His teachers include the late Terence McKenna, the still-popular mystic/ethnobotanist, and the late Anne and Sasha Shulgin, the psychedelic chemist and "Godfather of Ecstasy."

"I was trying to understand how consciousness worked. What is being? What happens when your ego dissolves and all of time and space are present? The Christian churches in Tennessee were not helping me make sense of the experiences I was having with these entheogens. Maybe a little, with Jesus talking about love. My family was more of a seeking family than a knowing family, but we had our creed. My brother Daniel, a very observant Anglican Christian, would ask me things like, 'Does your God have a personality, a character you can relate to?' I'd say. 'Yes but the God of that mystical experience is a God that is truly beyond words and beyond the capacity to ever be defined. God is everything—probably even a man on a throne in the sky for all I know. God has the personality of all personalities. My guess is that God will relate to me in whatever way I am capable of relating to him or her.'"

Bob's inability to find answers in the church in Tennessee inspired a five-month pilgrimage to India in the 1980s, but he was mostly disappointed with the ashrams and gurus he encountered there. Today, he does not apologize for taking short cuts to nirvana via psychedelic drugs and sacred plant medicines. "Sure," he says, "I could spend my life doing mindfulness meditation, and I'd make some progress, but I'm confident that I would never have had the kind of experiences I've had with LSD or DMT."

According to his community's public website, the "etheric body" of this church was founded "at the beginning of time." It has been a "practicing group" since 1984, an apparent reference to a small group that formed after Bob's LSD revelation as a teenager back in the Smoky Mountains. Sacred Garden was officially founded as a non-profit church when its organizers filed papers with the state of California in April 2020.

Between forty and sixty congregants attend weekly Sunday services—some via Zoom and some at a rented light-filled sanctuary on the Oakland/Berkeley border. Like all churches, Sacred Garden struggled to keep operating during the COVID-19 pandemic. There were heated debates and some defections over masking, vaccination rules, and testing requirements.

Sacred Garden has a board of elders and an independent ethics council designed to ensure that church leaders have accountability and operate in an ethical manner.

During my months as an active church member, Sacred Garden Church formally ordained a half-dozen ministers, also known as facilitators. Some were mostly trained by indigenous teachers in Latin America. Others graduated from an underground psychedelic therapy training program led by Aharon Grossbard and his wife, Françoise Bourzat. In 2021, that couple was publicly accused by former students and colleagues. of nonconsensual sexual touching and unethical romantic relationships. [2] They declined in an email exchange to respond to those allegations in this book.

Sacred Garden seems to have learned some lessons from the controversies surrounding Bourzat and Grossbard. Members who experience what they see as inappropriate behavior are encouraged to report it to an independent ethics council at the church and, failing that, to auditors working with the Sacred Plant Alliance. Other Sacred Garden clergy have been certified in psychedelic therapy in an above-ground program run by California Institute of Integral Studies in San Francisco. Regardless of their background, ordained Sacred Garden facilitators go through additional training in the ethics, safety and mental health considerations involved in the use of various drugs and plant medicines.

Sacred Garden Church is a strange, psychedelic brew of legalization advocates, underground therapists and sincere spiritual seekers. To seasoned observers like Rick Strassman, the Jewish DMT researcher we met in chapter two, this emerging congregation is an example of how "the psychedelic renaissance is experiencing growing pains in its adolescence."

"Hype is giving way to a more measured assessment of claims with increasing data derived from rigorous studies as well as greater sophistication in designing and performing studies," he said. "But I'm concerned that the rush to increase access is based more on advocacy and less on convincing clinical data. This push to increase access for 'therapeutic purposes' that undergirds the legalization and decriminalization movements seems to be a screen for promoting increased recreational use, often-times for financial gain. Increased access means increased adverse effects and these may derail more formal adoption of psychedelics within the mainstream. That is, if increased access leads to a public health emergency as it did in the late 1960s and early 1970s, the DEA—regardless of FDA's determination of therapeutic utility—will have to step in and tighten enforcement of existing scheduling laws."

Like many new churches, Sacred Garden is searching for a long-term economic model that will sustain it and provide access for low-income people. Seed money to get the church organized and provide modest salaries for a couple of staff members was donated by David Bronner, the drug reform activist, psychedelic therapy philanthropist and "cosmic engagement officer" at Dr. Bronner's All-One Magic Soap Company. Members of the church are asked to donate monthly, and to pay additional amounts for ceremonies like the changa initiation ceremony or individual or small group sessions run by its ordained facilitators, some of whom also work as freelance guides apart from their role in the church. During my time with the congregation, Bob and a small core group of members were working to design longer ceremonies and retreats where new members can engage in deeper entheogenic exploration, such as a Heart Opening" ceremony that employs MDMA.

Churches and mystical movements are notoriously schismatic, and Sacred Garden is no exception. There have been debates and divisions around gender, sexuality and identity politics. One leader left over the church's connections to Mimosa Therapeutics, a start-up company using a new approach to grow and package psilocybin. Since you can pretty much believe anything you want, church members are free to offer all kinds of testimony about their psychedelic revelations. Some may think the entities they see on DMT are real. Others are true believers in astrology or seek to promote the latest miracle cure for all that ails us. Meanwhile, Pastor Bob gently shepherds his free-thinking flock as best he can, letting members define the divine as they see it.

"Sacred Garden Church is not a political action group," Bob told me. "We're not going to be a right-wing anti-abortion church or a left-wing anti-capitalist church. We just wanted to grow community around these plant talks, to let go of the things that cause us to be mean or hateful or abusive to each other. You come here and receive soul medicine, to enter into a numinous experience of what is real."

SARA MORRILL WAS BORN on a U.S. Air Force base in Mesa, Arizona in 1991, two days before the Fourth of July. Her parents, grandparents and great-grandparents were conservative evangelical Christians going all the way back to an ancestor who came over on the Mayflower.

Growing up, Sara and her siblings attended Baptist, Calvinist and non-denominational Christian congregations.

Around the age of twelve, Sara started feeling "a little outside the box in my faith."

In Sunday school, she'd been showed the "Left Behind" videos, a dramatic series about how the End Times were coming and only the faithful would be raptured. "I was afraid that people in my life would disappear from earth and that I wouldn't be chosen to go to heaven."

After college, Morrill landed a job working at a holistic treatment center in Hawaii that used horticultural therapy to help adolescents struggling with mental health issues. "I was holding space for kids and teens," she said, "but I wasn't doing my own inner work."

It was there that she heard about a retreat center in Bolivia that was promoting ecologically oriented tour groups dedicated to preserving the rainforest. There was a job opening, so Sara headed south.

After she arrived at the retreat, deep in the Amazon jungle near the Brazilian border, Morrill decided to participate in plant medicine ceremonies offered there. At the time, she was struggling with chronic fatigue and food intolerance. "I was seeking spiritually," she said. "I wanted to heal my health and feel connected to myself. I knew to really explore this part of me I needed to go somewhere else, far from the culture and identity I was used to."

When we spoke, she'd had twenty-eight journeys on ayahuasca and other psychoactive plants. Sara looks back on those first ceremonies as "real life-changers."

"I traveled inside the blocks in my body. I cried a lot of tears. A lot of it had to do with my orientation toward God and others, and having this whole identity to serve other people, while believing I wasn't worth that myself. My service toward others wasn't coming from a place of love. But this was so intense and so beautiful and so big. It was like everything I'd known up to that point was a lie."

Coming home and explaining all this to her parents was not easy. "When I went back home, I was very angry and sad. It was hard to go back to my family and be invited to church. It didn't feel honest for me to go. I did tell my parents [about the ayahuasca experiences]. They'd say, 'You're doing drugs. People who do drugs end up homeless and addicted and live under bridges.' At that time, that was very hard for me to figure out. They were begging me not to go back to South America. They'd say, 'Please, can't you go with a Christian organization?'"

"My dad sat me down with a Bible and said, 'No truth ever came from taking a substance.' He was coming from a really loving place, and tried to be tactful with his words. But it was hurtful and confusing at the time."

In recent years, Sara has tried to reconcile her psychedelic experience with the religion of her ancestors. She's now come to see both as "holy and sacred." She has come to see that "this is what my parents were trying to give me. They may call it Jesus. To me, it is pure source energy. They were trying to give me something I already had."

Morrill went back to the jungle and lived there for a year. She sought to deepen her psychedelic insights into non-duality with a yoga practice, meditation retreats and working with indigenous people.

"Mother Ayahuasca speaks to you in a language you understand. She shows me what is already inside of me. I'd go back to the things I was taught as a kid about Jesus and the Holy Spirit. Growing up, we put God in a box. Jesus was this white male figure who is my savior. I now see Jesus as a fully awakened person. I connect with the energy of Jesus. That energy is inside me. It's like the essence of Jesus. It doesn't matter if he existed or not, or if you believe he existed."[3]

Flash-forward a few years to another circle of psychonauts in another stand of trees. Sara Morrill was leading five congregants—myself included—in a plant medicine ceremony. We're not in the Bolivian jungle. We're in Redwood Regional Park, in the Oakland hills across the bay from San Francisco. We're not drinking ayahuasca tea, but we are smoking a dried blend extracted from the same psychoactive plants that power that entheogenic brew.

Morrill was the youngest of a half-dozen ordained ministers shepherding the flock at Sacred Garden Church. During my first visit to the church, back in the summer of 2021, I'd met one of the oldest members, someone from my generation.

Dr. Gary Kono, a member of the Sacred Garden board of elders, was in his early seventies. A retired dental surgeon, he grew up in Berkeley, where he studied at the University of California during the Free Speech Movement, and at UCSF at the height of the Haight/Ashbury scene. Unlike me, Gary did not experiment with psychedelic drugs during his early years in Berkeley and San Francisco. He bought into the anti-drug propaganda of that era, about crazed acid heads jumping out of windows. He didn't explore psychedelics until after his retirement, after his parents died, and his kids left home. Bob Stanley began mentoring him about plant and fungi entheogens. In December of 2018, Gary, Bob and others brought together the group that successfully convinced the Oakland City Council to decriminalize some entheogens in Oakland.

When we first spoke, Sacred Garden was one of many churches in the Bay Area that was just starting to resume in-person services after a long COVID-induced lull. Gary and I stood off to the side as about two dozen church members filed into their sanctuary. Another couple dozen members and potential members tuned in via Zoom, their faces projected in little squares on a large screen. As the service was about to start, Gary told me how he'd always been "a poster boy for external success, but deep down I felt very lonely and disconnected."

"Through entheogens I've had divine experiences. I lost my fear of dying. Most of the time, I'd been in the paradigm of the ego—planning the future, worrying about the past. Entheogens brought me to the paradigm of this moment. Right now. Our true selves dwell in the now. Not in the ego."

Bob and Gary had originally agreed to let me use their names and the name of the church in a freelance story I was writing about emerging psychedelic churches in the Bay Area. But at the last minute they changed their minds and asked to remain anonymous. I revised the story, and with a bit of snark called Sacred Garden "the Church that Dare Not Speak Its Name—at least in the pages of the *San Francisco Examiner*."[4]

In early 2022, I reconnected with Bob and agreed to follow the protocol required to formally join the church. Like all prospective members, I spent three months in preparation, going to Sunday services where no psychedelic sacraments are served, but where members of the church offer testimony, seek to calm the mind through various meditation and visualization techniques, and listen to Bob's "Plant Time" sermons.

This all led up to my initiation on that Sunday afternoon in Redwood Regional Park. Stanley was with us, helping Morrill learn the still evolving liturgy of this emerging church. I've attended nine of the Sunday services, along with a series of church workshops where initiates are given tips on how to incorporate entheogenic insight into their daily lives.

A few Sundays before this ceremony, I stood before my newfound brethren and recited what passes for a creed in this little experiment in psychedelic communion: *We are open to the possibility that, engaged through careful and respectful practice, entheogens can connect us to direct experience of the divine, within this lifetime.*

Today's sacrament is changa, the dried leaves of plants that are native to the Amazonian basin, but that Bob now grows in his own garden. Changa is smoked, not drunk, so the psychoactive effect is more immediate and much shorter acting. Like ayahuasca, changa contains naturally occurring DMT.

Preparation, intention, and integration are the pillars of the psychedelic renaissance. For me, this is also a way to convince myself that I'm not just "getting high," that I'm not just doing this recreationally, for kicks, but for some higher purpose. That might be a form of psychotherapy or self-care designed to address a particular trauma, mood disorder, such as depression, or behavioral disease, like alcoholism. Or it might be more of a spiritual quest, an attempt to promote a more compassionate and less self-centered approach to life, or to connect with God, Ultimate Reality, or a non-ordinary, "non-dual" state of consciousness where the boundaries between self and other miraculously dissolve.

We start this four-hour afternoon journey sitting in a circle on a little bluff above the Redwood Regional parking lot. Stanley rings a bell and Morrill leads us in a short meditation, focusing on our breath. Then we are each invited to state our intentions for the ceremony.

One of the other initiates, a friend of mine named Jose, talks about how he felt "stuck in a downward spiral of inaction." As a young man back in the 1980s, he'd had a "life-changing experience" on LSD. That trip showed him "an alternate reality in which my ego dissolved," opening up a new way of thinking. He'd joined Sacred Garden Church to rekindle that expanded state of consciousness and find a "renewed sense of hope."

Once everyone speaks for a few minutes about our hopes and fears for the impending journey, we get up for a 45-minute hike to a secluded redwood grove. We enter in silence, proceeding off the main dirt road, then down a hidden path, and finally cross-country farther down a steep ravine. I'm the oldest psychonaut in the group, and not in the greatest shape, so just getting down to the grove without tumbling down the hill was my greatest challenge. Andre, one of the founding church members who is here to assist Bob, senses my distress and kindly sticks by my side, catching me before one potential fall.

Once we arrive at the grove, we unpack the provisions we were told to bring—a blanket or some kind of cushion, along with our own pipes, cigarette lighters and a few cherished items to place on cloth altars. Stanley arranges some bells and small sound bowls on the cloth laid down where he sits.

Another founding member of the Sacred Garden quietly walks around this circle of psychic explorers, filling our pipes with a sprinkling of the dried brown material. Then Stanley holds up his pipe, signaling that it's time to fire up our bowls and take the first of three tokes. It's a windy afternoon, and my lighter is no match for the stiff breeze blowing through our sacred circle. Morrill senses my frustration and comes over to help me set my little bowl ablaze.

It only takes five to ten seconds for the changa to start working its magic, just long enough for me to close up my pipe and set it down on a damp cloth I brought along to minimize any chance of starting a fire. With eyes closed my consciousness shifts into another realm, rushing back into itself amid swirling, kaleidoscopic patterns of the deepest, most wonderful shades of purple I've ever seen. I'm still me, but my every day, egocentric self soon quiets down into a kind of blissed-out serenity.

Time stops, but at some point, I lay down on my blanket, rest my head on my day pack and gaze up into the redwood canopy. There's a peaceful stillness to the forest that passeth understanding. Leaves, firs and ferns dance and glistened with a life-force one normally does not see. I hear some gentle moans, a few "ohs" and "ahs" from the others, reminding me that I am not alone. But, too quickly, my old monkey-mind returns and starts turning the experience into a story, the tale you're reading right now. Then the skeptic chimes in. "Is this really so special? What's 'the divine' got to do with it?"

After my third and deepest toke, I lay back down and try to put away the doubt. Morrill has a small drum with her and she begins to sing an *icaros*, a sacred hymn to Mother Ayahuasca. They say "music fuels the medicine," and that is certainly happening on this Sunday afternoon. As a beam of light shoots through the trees, my mind opens, my judgments drop, and this young medicine woman sings an angelic song.

Tierra es cuerpo (Earth is my body)
Agua es sangre (Water is my blood)
Aire es aliento (Air is my breath)
Y Fuego mi espiritu (And fire my spirit)

Of course, not all initiates to the Sacred Garden have only serene trips. One member recounted a terrifying experience after taking extra-large hits from his pipe. Everything around him froze in time, and the people he was with turned into one-dimensional characters, cartoon-like. One of the ordained facilitators at the ceremony sensed his distress and came over to comfort him. Having received prior consent to platonic touch for support, the guide took his hand to reassure him.

His story is an important reminder of something the psychedelic pioneers Aldous Huxley and Humphry Osmond pointed out way back in the 1950s, just as they coined the term: "To fathom hell or soar angelic, take a pinch of psychedelic." It's not all rainbows and bliss. Suddenly altering one's consciousness and sense of self, whether or not we do this "for a direct experience of the divine," can be emotionally upsetting and existentially challenging.

Another church member at one of the two Redwood ceremonies I attended was surprised at the intensity of the changa experience. We were told to take just a small inhalation the first time for a gentle "handshake" with the sacrament. "I would not call my experience gentle," this member told me. "I remember thinking on the first inhale, 'Wow, this is real magic! This is sorcery!' As if in the time-frame of one breath, I could be instantly transported into another dimension entirely, filled with vibrant colors, geometrical patterns, and partial loss of my regular ego state. I did feel the presence of an 'Other' as I have heard described in the DMT state. Who or what that Other is, I cannot say.

"At the end of the first round, as my experience of consensual reality began to be pieced back together, I felt a sense of shame at having a human body—probably something to dig into with my therapist. At the end of the second round, I found myself spontaneously bursting into tears. I had not been in any kind of melancholy state prior to the ceremony. When I discussed this in the integration conversation afterwards, I was told this is a good thing, that pent up energy can be released doing this work."

Bob Stanley estimates that about twenty percent of the changa participants "may report an experience of some challenging emotional content."

"Connecting with the divine is not always a pleasant,

euphoric, or blissful experience," he said. "We all carry suffering and alienation, as well as joy and insight. Our sacred practice can help us understand, learn and grow through that suffering and alienation. We can grow our capacity to experience who we are from a loving perspective, learn to let go of those behaviors that cause unnecessary suffering, and move more clearly and fully into divine presence."

CHAPTER 7
PSYCHEDELICS IN RECOVERY

If this were a twelve-step meeting, and not the last chapter in this book, I'd start out like this: *Hi, everyone. My name is Don and I am a recovering addict and a semi-retired journalist.* It has been more than sixteen years since I touched the three drugs that were making my life unmanageable—vodka, cocaine and the daily newspaper business. Hopefully, I'd get a laugh from the dozen people sitting around a table in some dingy church basement.

At most twelve-step meetings—such as those listed in the directories of Alcoholics Anonymous, Narcotics Anonymous or Cocaine Anonymous—I would be extremely reluctant to expand on that introduction with the following postscript: *About eight years ago, I carefully and cautiously tipped my toe into the therapeutic and spiritual use of psychedelics, partly for greater insight into my own melancholy, anxiety, and addictive mind, and partly as research for a book about the psychedelic renaissance.* I would be reluctant to reveal that wrinkle at a regular AA meeting because most twelve-step groups today still preach an abstinence-only approach to all mind-altering substances. But there is a notable exception to this rule. It's called "Psychedelics in Recovery," a support group I helped get off the ground, partly to remind us that Bill Wilson, the co-founder of Alcoholics Anonymous, would have felt right at home in our new-fangled fellowship.[1]

PIR is open to alcoholics, drug addicts, or others struggling with destructive behavior around food, sex, shopping, work, or pretty much any obsession. Some members may gratefully credit a guided ayahuasca journey, mushroom trip, or other entheogenic experience with helping them achieve a long-sought state of sobriety in their lives. Others, such as myself, got sober the old-fashioned way—a stay at a rehab center, followed by a steady diet of twelve-step meetings and straight-talking breakfasts with fellow addicts and alcoholics in recovery. But we may have turned to psychedelics in search of greater insight into our addictive mind, to treat our continuing depression, or to deepen the spiritual awakening that's a central part of any twelve-step program.

Bill W. did not credit psychedelics with his sobriety when he and a friend, Dr. Bob, started their fellowship in the 1930s, but Wilson did turn to LSD in the 1950s in the hope that it would help him with his lifelong struggle with depression. He was convinced that LSD could inspire some alcoholics to have a mystical experience that would set them off on a new life course. One of the foundations of the twelve-step recovery program Wilson and company devised in the 1930s is the proposition that alcoholics and other addicts must undergo a "spiritual awakening" inspiring them to "turn our will and our lives over to the care of God *as we understand Him*." Those are the only words in the twelve steps that were printed in italics, indicating an openness in the early AA circles, to finding God in Judaism, Christianity, Eastern spirituality, or, twenty years later, in a tab of acid. In fact, long before he discovered psychedelics, Wilson was a serious student of paranormal psychology and various forms of spiritualism, holding seances and other gatherings with some of the leading psychics of his time.

My journey with Psychedelics in Recovery flowed from the 2012 publication of *Distilled Spirits—Getting High, then Sober, with a Famous Writer, a Forgotten Philosopher and a Hopeless Drunk.* The book blends my own recovery story with a group biography of Aldous Huxley, Gerald Heard and Bill Wilson. It was also the beginning of my ongoing research into "the secret psychedelic history of AA." Two addicts who'd started a recovery fellowship in New York City, Kevin F. and Dmitri M., had invited me to participate in a public panel discussion about "Psychedelics and the Twelve Steps" at a venue on the Lower East Side of Manhattan. Several years later, I stumbled across Kevin and another addict-in-recovery, Todd Y., at a convention sponsored by MAPS, the pioneering psychedelic research and development outfit.

In 2017, I joined Todd, Kevin and a few other folks to put together a new online fellowship, Psychedelics in Recovery, or PIR. This was a few years before outbreak of the COVID pandemic and the explosion of Zoom meetings devoted to everything under the sun. Before the pandemic, our little group struggled to get traction, and I mostly fell away once I was convinced that our fellowship could soldier on without me. So did Kevin and Dmitri, at least for a while, leaving Todd and a handful of his associates to keep the flame going with one or two online meetings a month.

While COVID devastated many religious congregations and other spiritual fellowships, including psychedelic ones, it was a blessing for PIR and a godsend for this tiny-but-growing niche of recovering addicts who've found redemption through sacred plant medicines and their chemical cousins. As of this writing there are more than a thousand people on the mailing list and more than two dozen online or in-person meetings held every week. There's at least one other similarly named network that doesn't stick as close to the twelve-step recovery philosophy as we do. While my participation in PIR could be described as spotty at best, I have stayed close with a few of the founding members.

We'd heard pieces of each other's stories at meetings, over the phone, and whenever our physical bodies crossed paths. What is said at twelve-steps meetings stays at twelve-step meetings. But Todd did offer to share his story with me (and you) when I put on my reporter's hat and interviewed him over the same platform that has allowed PIR to blossom. It was an on-the-record Zoom conversation with a guy who (unlike me) respects the old AA tradition of anonymity.

Todd Y. was born in Germany in 1967 to two school teachers who worked for the U.S. Department of Defense. Both of his parents, who divorced when Todd was four, had roots in Pentecostal Christian churches. His mother returned to the states after the divorce and stayed active in the Assemblies of God denomination.

Bouncing back and forth between Germany and his mother's home in Missouri, Todd never felt quite at home at mom's church. He went up for the altar call at age fourteen, which he now remembers as a "genuine emotional stirring mediated by music and all the hypnotically repeated stuff." But as a teenager he was also reading books by authors like Carl Sagan. He couldn't swallow the church's rejection of evolution and other tenets of modern science. "They give you a stark choice. Either accept it as we are presenting it, or you might as well reject it entirely."[2]

So, at sixteen, Todd was "confirmed as an agnostic." That was the same year, in the mid-1980s, that he and some friends in Frankfurt started taking LSD and magic mushrooms. "We had a good time and I developed a fascination for psychedelics."

Unfortunately, Todd also developed a fascination for cocaine, alcohol, meth and heroin, to which he became addicted in 1988. He started trafficking in psychedelics to support his habit for hard drugs. "I had aspirations to be a musician, but was fixated around the needle and the spoon." The next fifteen years were not pretty. Treatment centers, AA meetings, jails, psych ward and eight months in prison. After prison, he found himself pushing forty, working as a waiter and living in his mother's basement in Missouri.

He tipped his toe—actually his entire body—back into organized religion in the summer of 2001. "I went to a Roman Catholic Mass every Sunday just to sit there. I'd feel a glowing golden light, which felt like the love of God, emanating from the choir." He was baptized as a Catholic in 2002, but it would be another seven years before he got clean.

That was the same year, in 2009, that he sat through his first ayahuasca ceremony with a shaman in New Mexico—a former high school math teacher with "a somewhat traditional Peruvian" approach. But Todd was not quite done with alcohol and opiates. A few months after his New Mexico pilgrimage he found himself back in Missouri, coming to in a local drunk tank. "It was there that the full teaching of the ayahuasca came forth," he recalled. "And it was there that, all of a sudden, I felt this great affinity for AA."

Still living in his mother's basement, Todd ordered dried plant ingredients from a mail-order house in Holland and started brewing his own ayahuasca tea. Using the twelve-steps of AA as a guide, he drank the brew three times a month for six months while working the steps with an AA sponsor. "He was aware of the ayahuasca, and was okay with it. He'd known me as drinker with track marks on my neck. I credit ayahuasca with giving me the inspiration to do all this. My mother was so impressed that she asked to drink ayahuasca with me. She wanted to understand how it had helped me."

After reading *Forest of Visions*, a book by the Brazilian Santo Daime leader Alex Polari, Todd joined that ayahuasca church in 2012, remaining active until 2019. During that time, he helped other addicts overcome their addiction with his home brew. "Even as a Daime member, AA and the twelve-steps was my real spiritual path. Santo Daime had the pageantry of worship, but the real structure was AA," Todd told me. "One of the things I've noticed in the psychedelic churches, including Santo Daime, is the tendency to become so heavenly minded that you're no earthly good. Working the twelve-steps reminds us to keep our feet planted firmly on the ground and to combat inflatedness."

Or, as the "Big Book" of Alcoholics Anonymous puts it, "Abandon yourself to God as you understand God. Admit your faults to Him and to your fellows. Clear away the wreckage of your past. Give freely of what you find and join us. We shall be with you in the Fellowship of the Spirit, and you will surely meet some of us as you trudge the Road to Happy Destiny."[3]

In recent years, Todd went on to form a non-profit organization called Recovery Nexus, which seeks to create recovery and personal growth environments that are supportive of psychedelic experiences. He also co-founded a spiritual care outreach program called Natura Care. All the while, he has remained a steadfast "friend of Bill."

BILL WILSON WAS BORN in Vermont in 1895 to parents who physically abused him and then abandoned him to his grandparents when he was ten years old. There was a history of alcoholism in the family. Bill's paternal grandfather, Grandpa Willy, was a ferocious drunk and a founding member of the East Dorset Congregational Church. His grandpa liked to tell young Bill about the moment of clarity in his recovery, when he climbed a mountain in Vermont, asked God for help, and saw a blinding light and felt an enlivening breeze. It was a story Bill Wilson would not forget.

After serving as a solider in World War I, Bill got a job in the 1920s as a stock broker and private investigator for some Wall Street businessmen. Bill's drinking problem escalated throughout the 1920s and into the 1930s. At the suggestion of an old drinking buddy, Ebby Thatcher, Wilson became involved with the so-called "Alcoholics Squad" of the Oxford Group, an evangelical Christian movement that was popular in that era. It was there that Wilson met another struggling alcoholic named Roland Hazard, a wealthy New Englander who had gone all the way to Europe to be treated by Carl Jung, the famous Swiss psychologist. Alcoholic Anonymous and its 12-step program grew out of the alcoholic recovery program of the Oxford Group. It expanded beyond the narrow confines of Christian conversion, in part, through Wilson's interest in the ideas of Carl Jung and his reading—at Ebby Thatcher's suggestion—of *The Varieties of Religious Experience*, the classic work by the American psychologist William James. In AA, Christian conversation was no longer a requirement for "spiritual awakening." In the 12-step program founded in 1934 by Bill Wilson and his new partner, an Akron, Ohio physician known in AA circles as "Dr. Bob," recovering alcoholics were instead encouraged to connect with a more open-ended "higher power."

So, how did we get from there, in the 1930s, to Bill Wilson dropping acid in the 1950s? Blame it on Gerald Heard and Aldous Huxley.

Heard was a once-influential Anglo-Irish writer, mystic

and philosopher and old friend of Huxley, the famous British writer who wrote a number of bestselling books, including *Brave New World* in the 1930s and *The Doors of Perception* in the 1950s. That latter book helped popularize psychedelic drug exploration a decade before anyone heard of Timothy Leary or the acid counterculture of the 1960s. Heard, who lived the last half of his life in Southern California, turned on *Time* publisher Henry Luce and his wife, Clare Boothe Luce, along with several leading theologians and business executives. He also inspired Dr. Oscar Janiger, a Los Angeles psychiatrist, who in turn turned on such Hollywood luminaries as Gary Grant, James Coburn and Jack Nicholson. Heard believed that the emergence of LSD in the twentieth century was simply God's way of giving us the gift of consciousness.

Gerald Heard was also the man who turned on Bill Wilson in the summer of 1956.

For two decades, Wilson had been a big fan and avid reader of Heard's many books about spirituality, meditation, mysticism and the evolution of human consciousness. The two men first meet in the early 1940s during Bill and Lois Wilson's first trip to California. At the time, Heard was running an eclectic spiritual retreat center in the mountains outside Los Angeles called Trabuco College, which Wilson visited on his journey.

More than ten years later, on another trip to California, Wilson had his first LSD session at the Los Angeles Veterans Administration hospital on August 29, 1956. Gerald Heard was his guide, and Dr. Sidney Cohen, an early LSD researcher, was the supervising physician. At the time, LSD was still legal. Everyone from psychologists to chemical warfare enthusiasts were looking for something to do with the mind-blowing drug that the Swiss chemist Albert Hofmann first synthesized at his Sandoz laboratory back in 1938, and then five years later realized what he had created. A group of researchers, including

Humphry Osmond, the man who turned on Aldous Huxley to mescaline, had successfully used LSD to treat alcoholism. At first, Osmond and his colleagues thought the drug would help them to better understand alcoholic hallucinations. It might terrify drunks to sober up. By the time Wilson had his first trip, Osmond had begun to see that it was insight, not terror, that was helping alcoholics mend their destructive ways. At first, it seemed counterintuitive. They were using one drug to overcome addiction to another. But they were doing what Wilson and AA had suggested in the second of their twelve steps. They were using mind-expanding drugs to find "a Power greater than ourselves" that "could restore us to sanity."

Wilson's thinking going into the session was that an LSD experience might help him overcome two of his remaining demons – his depression and his addiction to tobacco.

It's important for us to remember in our current enthusiasm for psychedelics that they didn't really work for Bill Wilson, at least for their intended purpose. Gerald Heard's hourly notes from the session reveal the trip did little to keep Bill away from cigarettes, a lifelong addiction that would kill him in the end. One of the first things he did was laugh and say, "People shouldn't take themselves so damn seriously." At 1 pm Wilson reported "a feeling of peace." At 2:31 p.m. he was even happier and proclaimed "Tobacco is not necessary to me anymore." At 3:22 p.m. he asked for a cigarette.

His depression lifted for a while, only to return when he got back to New York. "On my return home, I fell into one of my fits of exhaustion, which bordered on serious," Wilson wrote in a letter to Heard. Yet Wilson added, "I do not think that in any way my state is related to my experience in looking through 'The Doors of Perception.' In spite of my temporary condition, I do feel a residue of assurance and a feeling of enhanced beauty that seems likely to stay by me."

A few months later, Wilson was even more upbeat about the long-term benefits from the LSD session. "More and more it appears to me that the experience has done a sustained good," he wrote to Heard on December 4, 1956. "My reactions to things totally, and in particular, have very definitely improved for no other reason that I can see."

Other leaders in AA were aghast at Wilson's enthusiasm for LSD, and for years tried to conceal this chapter in the life of their founding father. Wilson defended his LSD use and psychic experimentations in a long letter written in June of 1958 – a statement that shows how his enthusiasm for the drug caused him to ignore its dangers. Wilson wrote that Osmond and his colleagues had given LSD to hundreds of subjects and there is "no record of any harm, no tendency to addiction. They have also found there is no physical risk whatever. The material is about as harmless as aspirin."

Father Dowling, a Jesuit priest who had known Wilson since the early 1940s, participated in at least one of the early LSD sessions in New York. He was initially as enthusiastic as Wilson, but would later warn Bill to be more careful with the drug. Some of the letters Wilson and Dowling exchanged between 1958 and 1960, the year Dowling died, talk of Wilson's ongoing psychedelic drug experiments. "On the psychic front," Wilson wrote on December 29, 1958, "the LSD business goes on apace...I don't believe that it has any miraculous property of transforming spiritually and emotionally sick people into healthy ones overnight. It can set up a shining goal on the positive side...After all, it is only a temporary ego-reducer...But the vision and insights given by LSD could create a large incentive – at least in a considerable number of people."

Nearly a year later, on October 26, 1959, Wilson wrote about the controversy the drug sessions had stirred up in AA, noting, "it must be confessed that these recent heresies of mine do have their comic aspects." He told Dowling, "The LSD business created some commotion...The story is that 'Bill takes one pill to see God and another to quiet his nerves.'"

Dowling replied by urging Wilson to proceed with caution. He even suggested that the devil might be working through LSD. Quoting St. Ignatius, the Jesuit priest wrote, "It is the mark of the evil spirit to assume the appearance of the angel of light."

Bill Wilson's enthusiasm for LSD is best expressed in his correspondence with the famous Swiss psychologist Carl Jung, In fact, the title of my book. *Distilled Spirits*, was inspired by a letter Jung wrote to Wilson in 1961. Jung was discussing how some diehard alcoholics must have a spiritual awakening to overcome their addiction. He pointed out that the Latin word for alcohol is *spiritus*. "You use the same word for the highest religious experience," Jung wrote, "as for the most depraving poison."

That letter of January 30, 1961— in response to a long letter Wilson wrote to Jung— is fairly famous in AA circles. But in my research, I discovered a second Wilson letter to Jung. In that letter of March 29, 1961, Wilson writes at length about his experiments using LSD to help members of Alcoholics Anonymous have the spiritual awakening that is central to the twelve-step program of recovery. "Some of my AA friends and I have taken the material (LSD) frequently and with much benefit," Wilson told Jung, adding that the powerful psychedelic drug sparks "a great broadening and deepening and heightening of consciousness."

Wilson told Jung that his first LSD trip reminded him of a mystical revelation he had after hitting bottom in the 1930s and winding up in a New York City hospital ward for hardcore alcoholics. "My original spontaneous spiritual experience of twenty-five years before was enacted with wonderful splendor and conviction," he wrote.

That spontaneous spiritual experience occurred in December of 1934 during Wilson's fourth and final stay at a private New York City hospital that employed something called the Towns-Lambert Cure to treat their alcoholic clients. Many of the patients were, like Wilson, once successful businessmen whose drinking had spun out of control during the Great Depression.

"Suddenly," Bill would later recall, "my room blazed with an indescribably white light. I was seized with an ecstasy beyond description."

That room was in a rehab center that employed a potion which included heavy doses of two drugs derived from plants known to cause delirium and hallucinations. One of them was belladonna, and the other, henbane, was long associated with witchcraft and potions said to summon the spirits of the dead.

So, in my opinion, it is *possible* that psychoactive plants played a *minor* role in what came to be known as the founding vision of Alcoholics Anonymous. I say minor because the entheogenic power of the herbs used at Towns Hospital pale in comparison to magic mushrooms or ayahuasca, or to the LSD Wilson would begin experimenting with two decades later.

My sense is Bill W's vision—which in its earlier accounts closely parallels the conversion story of Bill's alcoholic grandfather—was mainly caused as much by the delirium and ego deflation that comes when alcoholics stop pouring rotgut whiskey into their bodies and hit rock bottom. But perhaps the henbane in his Towns Hospital potion did help Bill W. commune with the spirit of his dead grandfather and have a vision that closely resembled the one he had been told about as a child.

Here's how Bill would later describe his Towns Hospital

vision: "In the mind's eye, there was a mountain. I stood upon its summit where a great wind blew. A wind, not of air, but of spirit. In great, clean strength it blew right through me. Then came the blazing thought, 'You are a free man.'"

In my view, it doesn't really matter if Bill's vision was caused by psychoactive plants, poetic license, or the workings of the One True God. What matters is that it transformed his life and inspired a crusade to free other alcoholics from the demon of addiction. By its fruits, we have come to know the power Bill W.'s vision.

In his second letter to Jung, Bill Wilson told Jung that many members of AA "have returned to the churches, almost always with fine results. But some of us have taken less orthodox paths. Along with a number of friends, I find myself among the latter."

Those friends included Aldous Huxley and Gerald Heard, who, like Wilson, were first attracted to LSD through their interest in seances, telepathy, spiritualism, other forms of psychic phenomenon and paranormal psychology.

In his letter to Jung, Wilson cited the Canadian research of Humphry Osmond. He reports that 150 hardcore alcoholics were "preconditioned by LSD and then placed in the surrounding AA groups."

Over a three-year period, they achieved "startling results" when compared to similar drunks who were not treated with psychedelics, but only got AA. "My friends believe that LSD temporarily triggers a change in blood chemistry that inhibits or reduces ego thereby enabling more reality to be felt and seen," Wilson told Jung.

Jung became seriously ill around the time he would have received Wilson's letter. He never answered the missive and he may not have even gotten a chance to read it before he died. But we know from some earlier letters that Jung was "profoundly mistrustful" that the average person could find lasting value from an LSD-induced glimpse into cosmic consciousness.

In a letter written in 1954 to a Dominican priest, Jung concedes that he knows "far too little" about the therapeutic value that mescaline or LSD might have for patients. "I only know," he says, "there is no point in wishing to know more of the collective unconscious than one gets through dreams and intuition."

Jung dismisses Huxley, who'd just published *The Doors of Perception*, as a hapless "Sorcerer's Apprentice," who has "learned from his master how to call the ghosts but did not know how to get rid of them again." A careful reading of Jung's 1954 letter to the Rev. Victor White shows that Jung's real concern was that LSD would overwhelm patients with a flood of revelations that they could not never fully integrate into their daily lives. He worried that this powerful new compound would become "a new poison to play with, without the faintest knowledge or feeling of responsibility."

Again, words of wisdom—especially for a fellowship of addicts considering the use of psychedelics as a tool in recovery. Jung wasn't even sure that *he*—the great Doctor Jung—was ready for an acid trip. "I should hate the thought that I had touched on the sphere where the paint is made that colors the world, where the light is created that makes shine the splendor of the dawn."

Jung died on June 6, 1961. Bill Wilson died on Jan 24, 1971 from diseases caused by the other addiction he could never shake—cigarettes.

A lot happened in the decade between the death of Carl Jung and the death of Bill Wilson. The sixties happened—a decade in which millions of psychonauts touched the spheres where the paint is made and the light is created. And many of us old-timers are still struggling to figure out what it all means.

It's unclear when Wilson stopped experimenting with LSD, which was outlawed by California on Oct. 6, 1966 (yes, 666) and soon after by other states. It was further criminalized nationally by the Controlled Substances Act of 1970, part of President Richard Nixon's "war on drugs." My guess is that Wilson stopped taking LSD in the early 1960s, just as drug was starting to become associated with beatniks, hippies and the psychedelic counterculture popularized by Timothy Leary and Richard Alpert. In a letter to Timothy Leary dated July 17, 1961, Bill Wilson wrote that Aldous Huxley had "referred enthusiastically to your work." Wilson goes on to write that "though LSD and some kindred alkaloids have had an amazingly bad press, there seems no doubt of their immense and growing value." The AA founder also hints that he knew of Leary's own problems with alcohol, adding that Tim might "find some interest in Alcoholics Anonymous—its principles and mechanism."

Leary's ouster from Harvard and his crusade to turn America onto psychedelic enlightenment is often cited as one of the reasons for the backlash against serious research into the therapeutic benefits of drugs like LSD, psilocybin and MDMA. There is some truth to that accusation, although the story is much more complicated than that.

In recent decades, psychologists and neuroscientists have resurrected substance abuse research that began in the 1950s and was shut down during the war on some drugs in the 1970s and 1980s. Clinical trials have, once again, shown the effectiveness of using psychedelic drugs, along with psychotherapy, to treat addiction to alcohol, cocaine and tobacco.

At the same time, there has been an explosion of interest in the ritualized use of ayahuasca, ibogaine and other plant medicines to help those addicted to various drugs of abuse. In one of my earlier books,[4] I interviewed addicts, alcoholics, therapists, shamans and scientists doing this work.

Carroll Carlson, an alcoholic treated in a clinical trial at the University of New Mexico, said a vision she had of Jesus during psilocybin-assisted therapy enabled her to "forgive myself for the choices I had made."

Gordon McGlothlin, a lifelong smoker approaching retirement, kicked his tobacco habit following a psychedelic clinical trial at Johns Hopkins University in Baltimore. Asked how his trip did the trick, he said, "You suddenly understand how your body and the universe are connected ... I might want to have a cigarette, but now I know I don't need it."

Carson, a heroin addict I interviewed at a treatment center in Mexico who asked that his last name not be used, was treated with two psychedelic medicines—ibogaine and 5-MeO-DMT. Carson, a 31-year-old evangelical Christian from Dallas, said he felt "reborn" after the experience. "Since the ibogaine," he told me, "the basic craving that I've had for opiates is gone for the first time in ten years."

If this all sounds too good to be true, that's because it sometimes is. Another heroin addict I interviewed went to this same clinic and quickly relapsed after his miracle cure. He soon realized that he needed an ongoing support group and other lifestyle changes if he was to stay free from addictive thoughts and behaviors.

That's exactly the point behind the Psychedelics in Recovery fellowship. As I mentioned in the beginning of this chapter, I got sober in 2006, and did so without psychedelics. In 2014, after eight years of taking nothing stronger than a double espresso, I started a new round of research and reporting on the psychedelic renaissance. Over the next eight years, I cautiously revived my own psychedelic experimentation. As a participant/observer, I explored the therapeutic and spiritual use of magic mushrooms, MDMA, ketamine, ayahuasca and 5-Meo-DMT.

Looking back, it seems obvious that the psychedelic renaissance and the twelve-step recovery movement would wind up sleeping together. Both grow out of brokenness, in ourselves and in American society. Both seek connection with a power greater than ourselves. And both are highly suspicious of any church, guru, or religious authority who tries to define our spirituality for us.

Religion scholar Stephen Prothero echoes this sentiment in a recent book about one of Wilson and Heard's close friends and colleagues, the pioneering Harper and Row religion editor Eugene Exman. Both AA and the "spiritual but not religious" movement, he writes, display "a mistrust of religious elites, hostility toward organized religion, acceptance of religious diversity, rejection of fundamentalism and strategically vague definitions of God."[5]

So far, in my own recovery, I have not touched alcohol and cocaine—nor have I fallen into the abuse of psychedelics. I still drink too much espresso. Others have not been so lucky. My work with Psychedelics in Recovery showed me how easy it is for addicts like me to fool ourselves and fall back into addictive, abusive and harmful use of drugs that, in a therapeutic or spiritual setting, might help us at least temporarily dissolve the ego and examine our own self-centeredness.

"Defining our own sobriety" may work for some, but certainly not for all addicts and alcoholics. Honesty, openness and truly knowing ourselves, with the help of a supportive community, seems to be the best route to recovery—with or without a psychedelic assist. It's especially important for those of us in recovery to approach these compounds with extreme caution—to be clear on our intentions, to know exactly what we are taking, and to do so with trained and trusted friends or guides. They are a catalyst, not a lifestyle. And they are certainly not for everyone, including many alcoholics and people addicted to other drugs.

Overcoming addiction is a long, perhaps a lifelong, process. Ultimately, as the religion scholar Huston Smith reminds us, our goal cannot just be achieving altered *states* of consciousness. As addicts, we know how easy that is. If our psychedelic journeys do not lead to altered *traits* of human behavior, what's the point? If psychedelics don't make us more kind, compassionate and connected, we are just fooling ourselves. We are—once again—just getting high.

CONCLUSION

Twenty of us—nineteen Native Americans and me—were gathered that night in a large tepee on a bluff overlooking the Navaho Nation, near what the white man calls Four Corners. Emerson Jackson, the president of the Native American Church of North America, sprinkled some water on a handful of dried cactus and molded the bitter medicine into two balls the size of strawberries.

"This is our sacrament," he said, directing me to wash the peyote down with an equally bitter psychedelic tea.

Sometime after midnight, amid the rattles of gourds, the guttural chanting of hymns and the steady pounding of drums, we entered another Reality. I gazed with new eyes across the circle. The peyote fans of two old women—kaleidoscopes of bright feathers and intricate bead work—took on pulsing luminescence. But it was not all bliss. There'd been a heated debate right before the ceremony began about whether I could join the circle. Jackson had invited me, hoping a newspaper story would help shift public opinion before an upcoming Supreme Court decision as to whether the Native American

Church was exempt from federal drug laws. But he had not cleared that in advance with the family that had organized the meeting. One of those two women had been arguing against letting me participate, leading to some feelings of paranoia on my part once the medicine started working its magic. But those feelings vanished when I looked into the glowing embers of the fire that had been lovingly tended to all night in center of the tepee. Suddenly, when the peyote priest blew on a whistle made from the bone of an eagle wing, the fire took on the form of a great bird that flew around inside the tepee, swooping up and out the hole atop this temporary temple, one of many erected that night across the vast Navaho reservation. At that moment, the woman who had been my nemesis lowered her peyote fan and flashed a subtle smile.

That encounter in the summer of 1989 was my first assignment as a religion reporter participating in a psychedelic religious ceremony.[1] It was the end of the "Just Say No" decade of the never-ending "war on drugs." Ronald Reagan, who led the West Coast campaign of the 1960s drug war as governor of California, was continuing that crusade as president of the United States. Some readers of the *San Francisco Chronicle* sent letters to the editor mocking me and denouncing the newspaper for publishing a story that referred to peyote as a sacrament. "Come on Chronicle!," one man wrote. "Let's have some responsible reporting. Our community is suffering terribly from the plague of Drug Addiction that is quite litterally [sic] killing us. Let's get over the 1969 Pro-drug mentallity [sic] of Timothy Leary and Don Peyote. You really should be ashamed for printing such an inane, destructive article."

More importantly, the U.S. Supreme Court would soon agree with those disgruntled newspaper subscribers. Less than a year after my story was published, the high court issued its ruling in a court case that would soon galvanize a broad spectrum of religious organizations and civil liberty advocates. It was a campaign that continues today in a broader fight for cognitive freedom. The 1989 case, known as *Employment Division, Department of Human Resources of Oregon v. Smith*, involved two members of the Native American Church who had been fired for using peyote and then denied unemployment benefits. In 1986, the Oregon Supreme Court had ruled that denial of unemployment insurance to Alfred Smith and Galen Black violated the men's constitutional right to practice their religion. The state of Oregon appealed that ruling to the U.S. Supreme Court. On April 17, 1990, it ruled in a 6-3 decision that the state's compelling interest to enforce drug laws trumped religious freedom. Writing for the majority, Justice Antonin Scalia called religious pluralism a "luxury" that must be sacrificed on the altar of the drug war. But the court's decision was quickly condemned by mainstream Catholics, Jews and evangelicals, who feared it could be applied to religious freedom cases that had nothing to do with drugs. "For all practical purposes," said Henry Siegman, executive director of the American Jewish Congress, "a majority of the Supreme Court has eliminated the free exercise clause of the First Amendment from our Bill of Rights." Congress responded to the controversial ruling in 1993 by passing the Religious Freedom Restoration Act, followed by a second law that gave even stronger protections to Native Americans.

Today, as we've seen in these pages, many other Americans are asserting their constitutional rights to use entheogens as a means to connect their psyche and their soul to a power greater than themselves. And we've seen that formal exemptions to federal drug laws are rarely given under the provisions of the Religious Freedom Restoration Act. This continued government resistance has inspired a new wave of political action to "Decriminalize Nature" and allow all Americans—

native or not—to use sacred plant medicines as part of their spiritual practice. Oregon, the state that brought the issue to the Supreme Court back in the 1980s, is once again center stage.

Peyote is also back in the center of the cyclone. Some in the psychedelic drug reform movement think cities and states should exempt the slow-growing cactus button from decriminalization, citing the fears of Native Americans about overharvesting and decimation of the desert peyote gardens in Mexico and the southwestern U.S. Others say the government has no right to criminalize any psychoactive plant for anyone, citing the concept of equal justice for all. Both sides make good points. Part of the problem, in my view, is drug reform efforts that limit decriminalization to entheogenic plants and fungi. Decriminalization efforts that include all psychedelic compounds—including MDMA, LSD, DMT, pharmacological psilocybin and synthesized mescaline—would give North American psychonauts options that threaten neither the peyote fields of Mexico nor the ayahuasca vines of the Amazon.

Other divisions have emerged over "cultural appropriation." Some argue that non-indigenous Americans should refrain from the ceremonial use of peyote or magic mushrooms out of respect for tribal cultures that used these plants and fungi long before the European invasion of the "new world." Again, I partly agree. There's a naive embrace of Native American customs across much of today's psychedelic renaissance, a romanticization that exaggerates both the extent and importance of entheogenic plants in indigenous cultures. It's easy to forget that the Native American Church is an invention of the late nineteenth and early twentieth century, formed around the same time that European chemists and assorted bohemians on both sides of the Atlantic were tripping out on mescaline sulfate. And we must also remember that Western

Civilization has its own entheogenic spiritual traditions dating back to the mystery cults of ancient Greece. Limiting magic mushrooms ceremonies to Mazatec Indians is a bit like saying only Swiss people should take LSD because the compound was discovered by a chemist working in Basel.

Nevertheless, the Native American Church *does* have something to teach those seeking to create new forms of entheogenic community. There is no distinction between "spiritual" and "therapeutic" in these rites, which arise in a real community of people with shared values and a common culture. It is not, like so much of today's psychedelic exploration, a one-off event in which the initiate spends a weekend at a high-priced retreat, or deep dives during a session with a pricey therapist. Again, there is nothing wrong with those approaches, nor with the recreational and celebratory use of psychedelics, which is how the vast majority of people structure the experience. But are those explorations something we can honestly call a "religion?"

Peyote ceremonies in the Native American Church are often called with a particular purpose—to pray for a sick child or to help a young man overcome an addiction to alcohol or other drugs. The Half Moon Ceremony I joined in the summer of 1989 was to help reconcile tensions in a family that was moving off the reservation. A man was taking his wife and three young children off to start a new job in Albuquerque. His extended family called the meeting to pray for his success and address his young wife's reluctance about making the move.

Speaking a mixture of Navajo and English, the young father spoke of his fears about the coming move, crying as his family and friends offered encouragement and prayers of support. His entire family was in the tepee throughout the night. The children, who were given small amounts of peyote, slept on colorful Navajo rugs. Intense waves of emotion and empathy permeated the proceedings. Time seemed to stop as the spirit of the peyote led the assembly into deep states of prayer, contemplation and healing.

Peyote rites in the Native American Church arose, in part, as a reaction to a couple centuries of cultural and genocidal war waged against indigenous tribes. The church was founded as a formal organization in 1918 in Oklahoma to fight off an anti-peyote campaign by government officials and Christian missionaries. "We use words like 'Amen' and 'Heavenly Father' and call it a 'church' so the white man can understand," Jackson told me.

In 1909, less than a decade before the church was organized, the federal Bureau of Indian Affairs sent out a questionnaire to government superintendents across the country. One of the most fascinating replies came from Indian agent Charles E. Shell, a superintendent for the Cheyenne and Arapaho Agency who had been known as a staunch peyote opponent. Before completing his questionnaire, Shell decided he should try the cactus buttons himself, so he did so in his own home under the supervision of a medical doctor. He reported that he experienced thoughts "along the line of honor, integrity, and brotherly love," adding "I seemed incapable of having base thoughts...I do not believe that any person under the influence of this drug could possibly be induced to commit a crime." He concluded, along with other officials who replied to the survey, that peyote used in religious ceremonies did not appear to be habit forming. In fact, there were numerous reports of it use as a cure for alcohol abuse among Native Americans.[2]

It was an honor for me to be invited into this intimate circle among the Navajo. Of course, I was an outsider and struggled with those feelings during my twelve hours in and around the tepee. There were moments of bliss, but also uncomfortable periods of paranoia. Like I said, not everyone wanted me to be there, and I did not feel particularly welcome. At one point during the night, I started to feel claustrophobic and left the tepee. Participants are only supposed to depart briefly if they need to leave the sacred enclosure to urinate. If you vomit, you do so sitting in the circle, and someone comes around to clean it up. When I did leave, ostensibly to relieve myself, I did *not* want to go back. I laid down on the ground and gazed up into the stars, a brilliant tapestry that was not above but all around me and within me. I was melting into the earth, feeling a magnetic connection of unity to all and everything.

My reveries were interrupted when the stern face of a young Indian man entered my field of vision. "You must come back," he said, pointing to the tepee. I returned and made it through the rest of the night. After sunrise, I declined the invitation to enter a small sweat lodge that had been constructed nearby, fearing that the heat and claustrophobia would just be too much. I said my goodbyes and walked over to my rental car, hoping to head out on the long and winding road to my motel in Farmington, New Mexico, about a ninety-minute drive. There I could do a little writing while the experience was still fresh in my mind and then get a little sleep. I hadn't been allowed to make any recordings or take any notes over the previous twelve hours. But when I reached into my pants pocket for the car key, my hand melted into my right thigh. I somehow managed to pull out the key, only to find my hand melting into the metal door when I tried to unlock the car. Perhaps, I thought, the peyote gods were trying to tell me something. Maybe I should stay at little longer rather than tackle the rough dirt road that winds down the bluff. I sheepishly walked back over to group of men who were sitting on the ground, sharing a box a cereal, and (at least in my mind) laughing at me. "Maybe I should hang out with ya'll a bit longer," I explained. "Too stoned to drive."

Such are the perils of psychedelic journalism. I was not on the Navajo reservation to write about my trip, but to offer my readers some insight into the workings of the Native American Church. My story would appear a couple days later on the front page of the *San Francisco Chronicle*, and get picked up via a wire service by other newspapers across the country. This was, of course, in the pre-Internet era, before everything anyone writes is instantly available to everyone in the world—at least to everyone with a laptop or a cell phone. This was also back in the days when reporters never, or at least rarely, referred to themselves in a mainstream news or feature story. "I" was considered a dirty word. We're in a very different world today, but I still find myself feeling like an outsider—a stranger in the strange land of the psychedelic renaissance.

In recent years, my forays into psychedelic journalism have been more consciously mixed with a personal search for therapeutic relief and spiritual communion. I've done better with the former than with the latter. My early experiments with ketamine and ayahuasca were done with the intention of better understanding that increasingly popular medical diagnosis known as "depression." While I did not get sober with the help of psychedelics, my experiences with sacred plant medicines in Brazil did give me deeper insight into the nature of my melancholy moods and addictive mind.

At one of our Sunday gatherings at Sacred Garden Church, Pastor Bob passed along an observation that rings true for me. "People use drugs, legal and illegal, because their lives are intolerable, painful, or dull. They hate their work and find no rest in their leisure. They are estranged from their families and their neighbors. It should tell us something that in heathy societies drug use is celebrative, convivial, and occasional, whereas among us it is lonely, shameful, and addictive. We need drugs, apparently, because we have lost each other."[3]

Sacred Garden Church, the "least dogma" congregation, provides space for twelve-step meetings for members who need to keep an eye on their addictive tendencies, as well as sponsoring its own social gatherings and community service work. What makes it a genuine religious community, in my mind, is the fact that its members regularly gather in fellowship to reflect in a sober (but not necessarily somber) way upon the nature of the entheogenic experience. The same can be said for the ayahuasca churches operating under the auspices of Santo Daime and União do Vegetal.

Of course, there are other less "churchy" ways for us to come together in entheogenic communion. In the summer of 2021, when I was first starting to think about this book, I ran into leaders of the Psychedelic Sangha of San Francisco, some of whom see Buddhism as a means to integrate and understand the psychotropic experience. This Bay Area tribe was more of a networking group than a religious congregation. It was fueled by the celebratory spirit of Burning Man culture, which emerged in 1986 around a bonfire on a San Francisco beach, and blossomed into a booming festival on the Black Rock Desert Playa north of Reno. Burning Man was originally envisioned as "an annual experiment in temporary community dedicated to radical self-expression and radical self-reliance." That spirit is easily traced back another two decades to three iconic events in the psychedelic counterculture—the San Francisco Trips Festival, the Human Be-In and the Summer of Love.[4]

Much of that same vibe—fueled by psychedelic drugs—enlivened the Psychedelic Sangha of San Francisco. It described itself as a home for "spiritual misfits, freaks, seekers, psychonauts, weirdos, rebels, outsiders, nonconformists, counterculturists, and anyone who elects to exercise their cognitive liberty."

"We don't provide psychedelic substances to people," said co-founder Christopher "Doc" Kelley, a Buddhist meditation teacher with a PhD in religion from Columbia University. "We provide a safe space for people to explore psychedelics and integrate the experience." Those spaces might include a gathering in Golden Gate Park or a visit to an exhibition at the Museum of Modern Art in downtown San Francisco. Members of the sangha (a word normally used to describe a Buddhist congregation) dose themselves, but "psychedelic rangers" are present to help anyone who has a bad trip. "We believe in the therapeutic benefits of recreational use. We've moved beyond the shaman paradigm. We empower individuals to make smart decisions."

For me, there's a lot to unpack in that little quote from the good doctor, and another quip from Kelley's friend and co-conspirator, the religion scholar Erik Davis. That would be his timely plea to "keep psychedelics weird." I ran into Chris and Erik at an event in Marin County, where all of us questioned the somewhat arbitrary divisions in the psychedelic scene between recreational, therapeutic and spiritual use. We all had mixed feelings about the medicalization of psychedelics and the accompanying rise of expertise and professionalism. "There's so much hype and emphasis on integration," said Davis, a popular speaker on the psychedelic circuit and the author of several books, including *High Weirdness: Drugs, Esoterica and Visionary Experience in the Seventies*. "People are pushing hard to find meaning. I like the lighter touch. I invite people to go into the mystery of these states, but mystery doesn't sell as well as a program or a plan."

Another psychedelic church I visited that summer of 2021, the Zide Door Church of Entheogenic Plants in Oakland, had a huge jump in membership following news stories about a police raid the previous year, which only shut down the operation for a day or two and resulted in no criminal charges. Zide Door, led by the very high priest Dave Hodges, looked more like a fortress than a church. It occupied the lower floor of an aging building on lower 10th Avenue, between International Boulevard and a homeless shanty town nestled along the BART tracks. Steel plates covered the inside of the windows. Members of the church passed by an armed security guard and through an airport-style metal detector. All visitors (including me) were required to join the fellowship in order to get past the reception desk and into the chapel. So I "joined," but did not leave with any mushrooms, nor have I since darkened its door.

Hodges grew up in San Jose, where he started his first cannabis club in 2009. He was running a bit late for our Friday afternoon meeting, which occurred the same week I first attended Sunday services at Sacred Garden. Hodges eventually arrived holding two giant clear plastic bags stuffed full of magic mushrooms. When we met, Dave was just shy of his fortieth birthday. "There is no doubt in my mind that mushrooms are the origin of religion," he told me. "At high doses, you leave your body and have spiritual visions and encounters with entities with lessons to teach you." He's a true believer in the "stoned ape" theory of religious evolution, an idea popularized by the Terence McKenna, the self-styled ethnobotanist and mystic. "Mushrooms help you connect with the part of yourself that exists outside of space and time," Hodges said. "Some call that soul. Some call that spirit."

Next to the small room where we spoke, rows of church pews that haven't been filled since the COVID shutdown were roped off with marijuana-leaf bunting. It had been well over a year since the high priest has given any sermons from the altar, which consisted of a pulpit surrounded by knee-high statues of the red-and-white-capped *amanita muscaria* mushrooms. But most of Hodge's flock prefer the popular (and safer) *psilcybe cubensis*. They can be obtained through the exchange of tokens, which are available to members who contribute to the good works of the church. Zide Door initiates are given a pamphlet with helpful tips on how to safely partake of the sacrament, whether they are microdosing to increase productivity or gobbling down mind-blowing doses to melt into divine oneness with all and everything. The first sentence offers some good advice. "Magic mushrooms are not for everyone." The safety guide ends with this warning: "Remember: MUSHROOMS CANNOT KILL YOU! They can only make you think they can. Everything will be ok."

It had been nearly a year since the Oakland cops seized $5,000 in cash and nearly $200,000 worth of cannabis and psychedelic mushrooms from Zide Door, but the authorities had yet to file any criminal charges. According to Hodges, the city was trying to shut him down by pressuring his landlord and declaring his church to be a public nuisance. But they were still in business, and the high priest told me his lawyers remained ready to fight for their constitutional right to commune with the mushroom gods.

In my mind, Sacred Garden appeared to be a more serious attempt to form a real community dedicated to the entheogenic exploration than Zide Door. There was more focus on safety, preparation and integration of psychedelic experiences at the Sacred Garden. While Dave seemed sincere in his spiritual quest, Zide Door looked more like a mushroom dispensary than a church. So, when I started doing my reporting for this book, Sacred Garden seemed like the place for me to go deeper.

Over the coming months, however, I began wonder

whether Sacred Garden was really a church for me at this stage of my life. The words of the late, great Alan Watts, the former Anglican priest and popular explainer of all things mystical, kept echoing in my head—something about hanging up the phone once you get the message.

Here's the full quote: "Psychedelic experience is only a glimpse of genuine mystical insight, but a glimpse which can be matured and deepened by the various ways of meditation in which drugs are no longer necessary or useful. If you get the message, hang up the phone. For psychedelic drugs are simply instruments, like microscopes, telescopes, and telephones. The biologist does not sit with the eye permanently glued to the microscope, but goes away and works on what he has seen."

In the end, none of these psychedelic churches—Santo Daime, UDV, Tom Pinkson's tribe, Sacred Garden, or even the Psychedelics in Recovery network—seemed quite right as a home base for *my* journey. Others, as we have seen, *have* found spiritual homes there. Maybe it's just that I am not, by nature, a joiner. In many ways, I feel like I have grown my own religion. Of course, I'm not the only one doing that. Millions of Americans reply "none of the above" when asked to describe their religious affiliation, or label themselves "spiritual but not religious."

Perhaps the main reason I declined to plant my spiritual flag in the Church of Psychedelia is that I'd already found a community that nurtures a divine connection within and without mainstream religion, with or without drugs, and, finally, within and without ourselves. For well over a decade, we have been meeting every Saturday morning at a retreat center in Oakland, or via Zoom during viral surges.

Our church, which has no name, started as a weekly meditation group organized by a small band of people—most of whom went to the same hospital-based rehab center for alcoholics and other drug addicts. But, from the very beginning, our group was also open to people who did not see themselves as formally "in recovery." And, from the start, the group was seen as a place for people of various faiths, or no faith. That said, we've always had a particular focus on Zen Buddhism and Christian mysticism, but not to the exclusion of other spiritual traditions. On one Saturday, we will sit for two short periods of meditation, listen to a talk by a Buddhist teacher who is also a recovering alcoholic and then talk about what's happening in our lives. On the next Saturday, we might augment our meditation sessions with a contemplative reading of a passage from the Gospel of Thomas, a brief missive from a medieval Christian mystic, or a Rumi poem. Two Roman Catholic priests who live at this urban retreat center, in a grand old house just up the hill from Oakland's Lake Merritt, are our hosts but not our leaders. Psychedelic drugs are never offered and rarely discussed—expect perhaps by me.

One of the reasons I stayed peripherally connected to Sacred Garden Church and the Psychedelics in Recovery network is those are more appropriate places to reflect upon the skillful use of psychedelics as part of a spiritual practice. For me, that would be my weekly session of Ketamine Music Meditation. Started as an alternative treatment for depression, this involves the slow sublingual ingestion of several ketamine lozenges, legally prescribed by a doctor and mailed to my home by a compounding pharmacy. My ketamine therapy began with an in-person session with my doctor, along with occasional visits to his office. This has not been the case with the later explosion of ketamine prescribing via "tele-medicine" during the COVID pandemic, which has led to recent reports of abuse and overuse of ketamine.

Over the years, I've come to see my in-home sessions as a

holy trinity of psychedelic use—therapeutic, spiritual *and* recreational. Therapeutic because I have found ketamine to be a better therapeutic treatment than traditional anti-depressants. Spiritual because I will *occasionally* fall into a mystical "non-dual" state of consciousness. Recreational because, like I said in the introduction, I really like getting high, and ketamine can take me there.

First thing in the morning, usually before sunrise, with eyeshades and headphones in place, I'll lay myself down in my studio and meditate to the accompaniment of a personal playlist of twelve evocative songs lasting a little over seventy minutes, never getting up until the music ends. Sometimes I will hardly feel any psychoactive effect. Other mornings, with the exact same dose and conditions, I'll experience a total dissolution of ego and connection to a metaphysical state of consciousness infused with gratitude, grace and an incredible lightness of being. It can feel, in a strangely comforting and occasionally frightening way, like dying. But I've come to see that what dies in this non-dual state is my small self, from which I become so disassociated that it completely disappears. That allows me to connect with a power greater than myself, a state of consciousness that is always there but hidden by the normal workings of the get-it-done mind. There are no visions or hallucinations, just a pure state of being rather than a busy state of doing.

One of the many mysteries surrounding this spiritual practice is the occasional nature of this intense mystical experience of unity. Sasha Shulgin, the infamous chemist who helped popularized MDMA, and cooked up a dizzying array of new designer drugs, calls this state a Plus Four (++++) experience that, by its very nature, cannot be reliably called forth. It is, in his words, "a rare precious transcendental state, which has been called a 'peak experience,' a 'religious experience,' a 'divine transformation,' a 'state of Samadhi,' and many other names in other cultures."

"It is a state of bliss, a participation mystique, a connectedness with both the interior and the exterior universes, which has come about after the ingestion of a psychedelic drug," Shulgin wrote. "If a drug (or technique or process) were ever to be discovered which would consistently produce a plus four experience in all human beings, it is conceivable that it would signal the ultimate evolution, and perhaps the end, of the human experiment."

Ketamine is not for everyone. My doctor says I am a particularly "good responder" to this medicine. Knowing its abusive potential, which is greater than other psychoactive compounds, I never take it more than once a week, as prescribed, and only in the manner I described. Yes, the antidepressive effect is temporary, but not as much as garden-variety selective serotonin reuptake inhibitors like Prozac or Zoloft. Ketamine does not alter serotonin, but triggers glutamate production in the brain, which allows the creation of new neural pathways that can allow for the production of more positive thoughts and behaviors. On rare occasions, I've had a frightening experience of existential dread, something we used to call a "bad trip."

Perhaps it's because I'm a religion reporter, and not a medical journalist, but it seems to me that the beneficial effects of psychedelics are better understood from a spiritual or ontological, rather than a scientific or medical, perspective. By "spiritual" I mean a radical re-envisioning of the self, leading to a connection with a power greater than ourselves, which we might call "God" or "Ultimate Reality" or even "Christ consciousness."

Let's end this exploration into the connection between psychedelics and religion with two of the twentieth century's most articulate interlocutors of East-meets-West dialogue—the aforementioned Watts and Brother David Steindl-Rast.

Alan Watts was born in a prosperous London suburb in 1915 and died in California in 1973. He dedicated his life to explaining some of the more ineffable aspects of Buddhism, starting in the 1930s with the publication of his first book, *The Spirit of Zen*, when he was just twenty-two years old. In the 1940s, he sought to deepen his understanding of his Christian roots by enrolling in a seminary in Illinois, getting ordained as an Episcopal priest, and accepting a call to serve as a college chaplain. In a 1951 letter to the famous Protestant philosopher Reinhold Niebuhr, Watts tried to correct the idea that Eastern mysticism's focus on "the void" made it a philosophy of negation.

"Negative language is used to relate, not to the real world, but the adequacy of all verbal symbols for the understanding of reality," he wrote. "We must know God as we know the tree, not by defining it verbally or conceptually…but by immediate perception. Thus the mystery of life is not seen as a problem to be solved but a reality to be experienced."

Watts returned to this theme in a 1959 radio talk on "Insight and Ecstasy." By then, his unconventional approach to love and marriage—perhaps inspired by his powerful love of drink—had forced him to leave the priesthood. He'd come out to California and fallen into the free-wheeling circles of Beat poets and other Bay Area bohemians. He'd also had his own psychedelic baptism. To me, the following quote explains why a single session of psychedelic-assisted therapy may instantly allow a patient or research subject to stop smoking, quit drinking or find sudden and seemingly miraculous relief from such medical conditions as depression or Post Traumatic Stress Disorder:

"One can't transform a sow's ear into a silk purse with a

dose of mescaline, but certain experiences of this kind might be valuable to people who are able to profit from them," he said. "There must be a distinction between ecstasy—the thrill and the kick, the delight and the joy—of a mystical experience and the experience itself...The experience is always a matter of insight. An understanding of the way things are and what you are and what life is may indeed produce ecstasy. Sometimes this experience is an immense relief. When one has been battling with some tremendous problem and one suddenly finds that the whole thing disappears. When you've been terrified with something or anxious and all the grounds for anxiety suddenly vanish, then very naturally you feel enormously happy and joyous. The kind of insight which is at the core of this sort of experience has a way of making the ordinary world seem extraordinarily beautiful. Before, things might have seemed dim and depressive...but now they seemed transfused with a divine light."

Amen, Alan. So many of our *psychological* problems are really false problems. "We are bothering our heads over questions that are not even real questions at all. When it is seen that we were asking the wrong question, then one gets this astonishing sensation of seeing that problems only exist in a mental sphere. They exist as a result of thought. The world is not thought. The world that simply *is* is entirely free from problems."

When Watts gave this talk at the Berkeley studios of listener-supported KPFA, the hippie counterculture had not begun to blossom in the San Francisco Bay Area. Back on the East Coast, Timothy Leary and Richard Alpert had yet to take their first trips. But Watts was already questioning the drug-induced mysticism of such Beat poets as Allen Ginsberg and Philip Lamantia, whose 1959 collections *Ekstasis* and *Narcotica* had inspired Watts' commentary. "Genuine mysticism is more likely to be found among humble and devoted adherents of such great traditions as Roman Catholicism or perhaps Buddhism as it is actually practiced in Asia," Watts said in that radio broadcast. "These are not people looking for ecstasy but devotees following a way of life which is often very hard indeed."

Watts' comments reminded me of one of my more precious memories during my years on the "God Beat." I was walking down a road above the Big Sur coast with Brother David Steindl-Rast, a Benedictine monk who helped put my own Christian upbringing in a new light.

Unlike some Christians we've met in this book, I am not in recovery from a fundamentalist, fear-based Christianity. I was baptized as an infant in the Presbyterian church in New Jersey. Growing up in Ohio, Colorado and Southern California, I was occasionally sent to Sunday schools in that denomination and in a liberal Congregational church. It was an experiment that ended at age twelve. Looking back, it seems like my father felt a responsibility to "expose" me to religion, but none of us in our family ever believed what we heard from the pulpit. In recent years, I've learned that my mother's reluctance to even discuss her Jewish heritage may have had more to do with the fact that—back in the Roaring Twenties—there were some serious gangsters and drug-runners in my maternal closet.[5]

My encounter with Brother David was in the early 1990s. I was on retreat—as a working journalist and as a human being—at Immaculate Heart Hermitage, a Roman Catholic monastery perched on a bluff over this spectacularly inspiring stretch of central California coastline. Brother David and I were not talking about psychedelics. We were talking about Jesus. Looking back on that conversation helps me reconcile my hidden Jewish heritage, my lapsed Protestant upbringing, and my entheogenic journey.

"When Jesus used scripture from the Hebrew Bible," Brother David told me, "it was not like the church does today. Jesus talked about *experience*, about daily experience. That was such an enormous change in a culture like that in Israel, where the idea of God was so strongly theistic. You know, Don, there is something happening in our time, and one of the most significant shifts is in the realm of religion. The emphasis is moving from the institution to personal experience. It is happening in people's lives on a very large scale, and it is absolutely irreversible."

I first experienced that shift in the fall of 1972, just before my nineteenth birthday, about ten miles up the coast from where Brother David and I would meet nearly two decades later. My first college girlfriend and I were sitting on a cliff, surrounded by sandstone statues carved to perfection by coastal winds. We had driven down from Berkeley, dropped two heroic doses of acid, and soon found ourselves melting into each other, then into the earth itself. At the time, that reality-bending encounter seemed to have had more to do with revelatory romance than old-time religion. But I've since come to see how my first full-blown mystical experience planted a seed that I have since tried to cultivate—with mixed success—into a new way of living.

It wasn't just Brother David who opened my heart, nor my young lover on that glorious day. It was this place. Big Sur can do that. For those of us who started on the East Coast and wandered across America in the decades following World War II, Big Sur was the end of the line. There was no more running from the past. There was nowhere to go but off the cliff or into yourself.

In 1995, just a few years after my encounter with Brother David at Immaculate Heart Hermitage, this monk was among a group of theologians, psychologists and entheogenic enthusiasts who gathered at a retreat center farther up the coast. His words at that seminar about the promises and pitfalls of psychedelic spirituality still ring true. "A genuine encounter with the Ultimate does not guarantee a genuine spirituality," he advised. "The experience may be authentic but how authentic one's spirituality will be depends on what the person who had the experience does with it. Will they allow it to transform their lives?"

"In whatever form we dare to approach the holy," the monk said, "we must always do so with fear and trembling. We must do everything we can to prepare ourselves. There is reason to fear overconfident blundering into the presence of a power that takes us beyond ourselves. Yet there is still greater reason to fear a timidity that shrinks from the experience of ultimate communion."[6]

Brother David was not saying that the stuff of organized religion—doctrine, ethics, ritual—are unimportant. But they only really work if they "give us fresh access to that primary experience from which they well up, as from their source."

"Even churches can become wastelands," he warned, "if they close themselves off from the living waters of the Spirit."

NOTES

INTRODUCTION

1. Lattin Don. *Distilled Spirits—Getting High, then Sober, with a Famous Writer, a Forgotten Philosopher and a Hopeless Drunk*, UC Press, 2012
2. www.lattinancestors.com
3. Lattin, Don. *The Harvard Psychedelic Club—How Timothy Leary, Ram Dass, Huston Smith, and Andrew Weil Killed the Fifties and Ushered in a New Age for America*, HarperCollins, 2010. p. 142

1. PSYCHEDELIC BAPTISMS

1. Interviewed on 2-1-22
2. Interviewed on 1-3-22
3. Talk at Harvard Divinity School webinar, 11-3-20
4. Interviewed on 2-17-22
5. https://faithlead.luthersem.edu/decline/
6. https://www.episcopalnewsservice.org/2020/10/16/2019-parochial-reports-show-continued-decline-and-a-dire-future-for-the-episcopal-church/
7. From a talk at Harvard Divinity School on 11-3-20 titled "Medicalizing Mysticism: Religion in Contemporary Psychedelic Trials."
8. Jay, Mike. *Mescaline—A Global History of the First Psychedelic*, Yale University Press, 2019. p. 40
9. *Harvard Psychedelic Club*, p. 73-84
10. Hofmann, Albert. "LSD as a spiritual aid," in *Psychoactive Sacramentals: Essays on Entheogens and Religion, Council on Spiritual Practices*, 2001, p. 121
11. Distilled Spirits, p. 186-190 and 200-204
12. Interviewed on 12-21-21
13. Strassman, Rick. "The psychedelic religion of mystical consciousness," Journal of Psychedelic Studies, 2018.
14. Lattin, Don. https://www.lucid.news/researchers-debate-the-role-of-mysticism-in-psychedelic-science/
15. Interviewed on 9-7-21
16. Lattin, Don. "Calling All Mystics: Clergy psychedelic study aims to awaken spiritual experiences," Religion News Service, 10-22-15
17. Smith, Dana G. "Psychedelics Are a Promising Therapy, but They Can Be Dangerous for Some," *New York Times*, 2-10-23
18. Interviewed on 3-21-22

19. Interviewed on 2-2-22
20. Interviewed 2-1-23

2. ON BEING PSYCHEDELIC AND JEWISH

1. The Pardes legend appears in various forms in the Jewish Talmud
2. Rifkin, Ira. "Ram Dass looks at Judaism again," *Tampa Bay Times*, 3-14-92
3. https://www.tikkun.org/the-torah-of-being-here-now/
4. Interviewed on 2-6-22
5. Lattin, Don. "Judaism's top thinker read Marx, then the Torah," *San Francisco Examiner*, 5-3-86
6. Interviewed 1-24-23
7. Interviewed on 1-12-22 and 1-30-23
8. Interviewed on 1-21-22
9. Interviewed on 3-21-22

3. MYSTIC CHRISTIAN REVELATION

1. Mabry is also the founder of Apocryphile Press, the publisher of this book.
2. Interviewed 3-28-22
3. Muraresku, Brian. *The Immortality Key: The Secret History of the Religion with No Name*, St. Martin's Press. 2020, p. 354
4. Interviewed on 1-16-23
5. Allegro, John M. *The Sacred Mushroom and the Cross*, Hodder and Stoughton, 1970, p. xv
6. Forte, Robert. "A Conversation with R. Gordon Wasson," in *Entheogens and the Future of Religion*, Park Street Press, 2012. p. 108-9
7. Wasson, R. Gordon. *The Road to Eleusis: Unveiling the Secret of The Mysteries*, North Atlantic Books, 1978, p. 29
8. *Entheogens and the Future of Religion*, p. 108
9. Riedlinger, Thomas J. "A Latecomer's View of R. Gordon Wasson," in *The Sacred Mushroom Seeker*, Park Street Press, 1997
10. Brown, Jerry B. and Julie M. *The Psychedelic Gospels: The Secret History of Hallucinogens in Christianity*, Park Street Press, 2016. p. 182
11. Published 8-21-70
12. Wasson, R. Gordon. Soma: Divine Mushroom of Immortality, Harcourt Brace Jovanovich, 1972, p. 179-80
13. Irvin, Jan. "The Secret History of Magic Mushrooms," cited in Brown.
14. https://cswr.hds.harvard.edu/news/2021/02/12/video-psychedelics-ancient-religion-no-name
15. Heinrich, Clark. *Magic Mushrooms in Religion and Alchemy*, Park Street Press, 2002, p. 206-7
16. Ibid, p. 105
17. *The Psychedelic Gospels*, p. 220-1

18. Interviewed 1-23-23
19. Interviewed 2-1-23

4. PSYCHEDELIC CHAPLAINS

1. Interviewed 2-6-23
2. Interviewed 3-28-22 and 1-16-23
3. Interviewed on 1-16-23
4. Interviewed 3-29-22
5. Interviewed 1-23-23
6. Lattin, Don. "Psychedelic Medicine," *Spirituality and Health Magazine*, September/October 2019, p. 37.

5. AYAHUASCA CHURCHES EMERGE

1. Interviewed 12-20-21
2. Interviewed on 1-5-22
3. https://www.lucid.news/plant-medicine-churches-legal-questions/
4. https://www.ayahuascachurches.org/
5. https://chacruna.net/chacruna_guide_rfra_best_practices_psychedelic_churches/
6. Interviewed on 8-16-22
7. www.lattinancestors.com
8. Interviewed 4-18-22

6. SACRED GARDEN CHURCH

1. Interviewed on 2-22-22
2. https://www.madinamerica.com/2021/09/ending-silence-psychedelic-therapy-abuse/ and https://www.thecut.com/2021/11/introducing-cover-story-podcast-trailer.html
3. Interviewed 3-31-22
4. Lattin, Don. "Psychedelic Spirituality: Inside a Growing Bay Area Religious Movement," *San Francisco Examiner*, 7-28-21

7. PSYCHEDELICS IN RECOVERY

1. https://www.psychedelicsinrecovery.org/
2. Interviewed 7-14-22
3. Alcoholics Anonymous, Fourth Edition, AA World Services Inc., 2001, p. 164

4. Lattin, Don. *Changing Our Minds—Psychedelic Sacraments and the New Psychotherapy,* Synergetic Press, 2017
5. Prothero, Stephen. *God the Bestseller*, HarperOne, 2023, p. 251

CONCLUSION

1. Lattin, Don. "Inside a Peyote Tepee—A Psychedelic Prayer Meeting," *San Francisco Chronicle,* June 19, 1989. p. 1
2. Stewart, Omer. *Peyote Religion*, University of Oklahoma Press, 1987, p. 142
3. Berry, Wendell. *The Art of the Commonplace: The Agrarian Essays,* Counterpoint, 2003
4. Lattin, Don. *Following Our Bliss—How the Spiritual Ideals of the Sixties Shape Our Lives Today*. HarperCollins, 2003. p. 120
5. www.lattinancestors.com
6. Steindl-Rast, Brother David, in *Psychoactive Sacramentals*, p. XII-X111.

ACKNOWLEDGMENTS

One barometer to measure the value of a psychedelic experience is whether it induces feelings of gratitude. As I type out this last page, I'm thankful to the many friends and colleagues who've allowed me to borrow bits of wisdom they discovered over the course of many lifetimes, and to weave them together into this modest work. Perhaps it's worth noting that I feel this gratitude without the assist of any psychoactive drug or sacred plant medicine, unless you count the double espresso that just jump-started my day.

Let me first thank my agent and former publisher, Mark Tauber, for sticking with me during times fat and lean; Ken Jordan at Lucid News for his early support for this project; and to John Mabry at Apocryphile Press for getting these stories from the Internet to the printed page, where I still feel most at home.

Thanks to the researchers, rabbis, pastors and psychonauts who've shared their stories with me, including Bill Richards, Roland Griffiths, Rachel Petersen, Tom Pinkson, Bob Stanley, and many others. Long lunches and Zoom calls with friends—including Mark Fromm, Tony Hoeber and David Roberts—inspired me to take this book home. My brothers and sisters in recovery circles, including Todd Y., Laura B., Jose S., Steve. F. and Kevin G., have helped me appreciate the wisdom of the twelve steps, which inform the final chapter of this book. My wife, Laura Thomas, has been at my side as a life partner, supportive critic, and sharp-eyed copy editor. My friends in the Lenox House Saturday morning meditation groups, including Fathers Don and Ray John, continue to provide space for a beloved spiritual community.

Printed in the USA
CPSIA information can be obtained
at www.ICGtesting.com
LVHW040304050923
757091LV00004B/458